THE PHONETICS OF FINGERSPELLING

STUDIES IN
SPEECH PATHOLOGY AND CLINICAL LINGUISTICS

AIMS AND SCOPE

The establishment of this series reflects the growth of both interest and research into disorders of speech and language. It is intended that the series will provide a platform for the development of academic debate and enquiry into the related fields of speech pathology and clinical linguistics.
To this end, the series will publish book length studies or collections of papers on aspects of disordered communication, and the relation between language theory and language pathology.

Volume 4

Sherman Wilcox

The Phonetics of Fingerspelling

THE PHONETICS
OF
FINGERSPELLING

SHERMAN WILCOX
University of New Mexico

JOHN BENJAMINS PUBLISHING COMPANY
AMSTERDAM/PHILADELPHIA

1992

Library of Congress Cataloging-in-Publication Data

Wilcox, Sherman.
   The phonetics of fingerspelling / Sherman Wilcox.
      p.   cm. -- (Studies in speech pathology and clinical linguistics, ISSN 0927-1813;
   v. 4)
   Includes bibliographical references and index.
   1. Finger spelling. 2. Grammar, General and comparative-Phonetics. I. Title. II.
Series.
HV2477.W55   1992
419--dc20   92-8926
ISBN 90 272 4334 4 (Eur.)/1-55619-390-4 (US)(alk. paper)   CIP

John Benjamins Publishing Co. · P.O. Box 75577 · 1070 AN Amsterdam · The Netherlands
John Benjamins North America · 821 Bethlehem Pike · Philadelphia, PA 19118 · USA

TABLE OF CONTENTS

Chapter 1
A Linguistic Approach
to Fingerspelling

The Structure of Signed Languages

"A language is a set of principles relating meanings and phonetic sequences" (Langacker, 1972:1). One type of phonetic medium is sound; one way of conveying language is through speech. Until recently, however, most linguists and researchers in the language sciences would have gone beyond the characterization of sound as a possible phonetic medium and would have insisted that more than being "merely one way of conveying language, the sounds of speech are, instead, its common and privileged carriers" (Liberman, Cooper, Shankweiler, and Studdert-Kennedy, 1967:431).

It is certainly true that in approaching the study of language, the data most readily at hand come from speech. Spoken languages are all around us; sounds are clearly a common way of representing meanings. But are they privileged? We must be careful about making claims concerning language in general on the basis of a particular language. If we examined only English, for example, we might conclude that relatively strict word order is a property of all languages. Cross-linguistic data are necessary in order to get a full picture of the structure of human language.

Just as important are cross-modal data. Linguists now recognize another medium through which languages can be conveyed. Numerous natural languages exist which are represented in the visual-gestural modality. Research has established that these signed languages[1] are fully independent of spoken languages. The most extensive research to date has examined American Sign Language (ASL), the signed language used by deaf people in America (Bellugi and Studdert-Kennedy, 1980; Fischer & Siple, 1990; Grosjean and Lane, 1980; Klima and Bellugi, 1979; Siple, 1978; Wilbur, 1987).

For many years, signed languages were thought to be dependent on spoken languages. In particular, ASL was considered to be merely a derivative of English. One explanation for this misconception can be found in the distinction between languages and modalities (Table 1).

Table 1: The Language/Mode Distinction

Language	Mode
English	
Spanish	Speech (Spoken Language)
Cochiti	
French	Writing (Written Language)
American Sign Language	
French Sign Language	Signing (Signed Language)
British Sign Language	

Speech is the primary means of representation for most natural languages. Written languages are usually characterized as secondary systems used to represent spoken languages in a written form, for particular purposes such as overcoming the temporal or distance limitations of speech (Gelb, 1963).

Table 1 can be used to explore the relationships among languages and their modes of representation. English, Spanish, and French, for example, are both spoken and written. Cochiti, like many of the world's languages, has no conventional written form. American Sign Language has no conventional spoken or written form; its only means of expression is through the signed modality.[2]

Since speech — spoken language — was for so many years viewed as primary and the written modality as secondary, it was perhaps natural for linguists to suppose that the signed modality was likewise used as only a secondary medium for the representation of spoken languages. What must be recognized is that the signed modality can serve as the primary medium for a set of natural languages.

Signs as Unsegmentable Wholes

As for our understanding of the phonological structure of signed languages, the common belief for many years was that the words of signed languages, unlike the words of spoken languages, had no internal structure. Signs (words) were regarded as unanalyzable wholes. Thus, a word such as LIKE (Figure 1) was regarded as a wholistic item, an unanalyzable gesture, with no internal structure.

Figure 1. The ASL Word LIKE

Signs as Simultaneously Segmentable

It was not until the publication of the classic monograph, "Sign Language Structure" (Stokoe, 1960), that this conception was refuted. Stokoe noted that signs, like words, do have an internal structure by demonstrating that signs must be described in terms of three parameters: *dez* (hand configuration), *tab* (location), and *sig* (movement). Stokoe originally coined the term *chereme* for these sublexical units, but later researchers pointed out that what was being described was the phonological structure of ASL and preferred to call them phonemes. Working within Stokoe's framework, researchers began in earnest to study the phonology of signed languages (Battison, 1973, 1974; Battison, Markowicz, and Woodward, 1975; Friedman, 1976; McIntire, 1977; Wilbur, 1985).

As an example of how Stokoe's three parameters can be used to describe the phonology of ASL, it is instructive to consider minimal pairs. Varying only the handshape parameter, it is possible to sign the minimal pair ONION and CHINESE. Varying only the location parameter, we can sign the minimal pair CHINESE and BORING. Varying only the movement parameter yields the minimal pair NAME and SHORT. A fourth parameter, orientation, was suggested by Battison (1973; Battison, Markowicz, and Woodward, 1975). Varying only the orientation parameter yields the minimal pair TRAIN and SHORT.

As research proceeded under this view of sign structure, linguists began to note that the structure of signed and spoken words differed in one remarkable way. Unlike spoken words, in which phonemes are arranged sequentially, the phonemes of signs are simultaneously present. As Stokoe noted (1960:37):

> The sign morpheme, however, unlike the morpheme or word of a spoken language, is seen as simultaneously, not sequentially, produced. Analysis of the sign morpheme then cannot be segmentation in time but must be aspectual.

The different sublexical structure of signs and words — simultaneous versus sequential — was taken as evidence for how languages are differentially structured by their modality (Bellugi and Studdert-Kennedy, 1980). Klima and Bellugi (1979:39) succinctly present the argument:

> Thus the lexical items of ASL and all other primary sign languages we know of appear to be constituted in a different way from those of spoken languages: the organization of signs is primarily simultaneous rather than sequential. ASL uses a spatial medium; and this may crucially influence its organization.

Signs as Sequentially Segmentable

Recent phonological research on American Sign Language is suggesting that signs are not only analyzable simultaneously but also sequentially (Liddell, 1984a, 1984b, 1990; Liddell and Johnson, 1986, 1989; Padden & Perlmutter, 1987; Perlmutter, 1990; Sandler, 1986, 1989, 1990; Wilbur, 1990). Liddell, for example, argues that signs can be sequentially analyzed into Movements (M) and Holds (H). Under this analysis, the sign LIKE consists of three segments (HMH), as in Figure 2.

The initial H segment is defined by several features; for the sake of simplicity, only a few are depicted in Figure 2 and only the handshape parameter is given values. In Liddell's analysis, autosegmental feature spreading would account for the M-segment features.

Liddell's model of ASL phonology has been developed in great detail. Presenting evidence from word formation and compounds, and drawing on work in spoken language autosegmental phonology, he convincingly demonstrates that the phonological structure of signs is more similar to that of spoken words than was previously thought.

Sandler (1986) has proposed an alternative autosegmental model of ASL phonology. In her model, the opposition is not between movements and holds but between movements and locations, with handshape on a separate autosegmental tier;

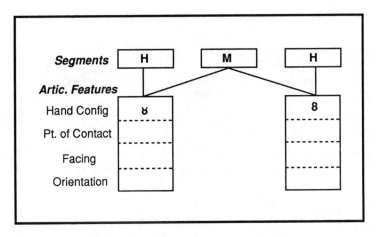

Figure 2. Autosegmental Analysis of LIKE

holds are represented as a binary feature of location. Sandler's model offers perhaps a more satisfactory explanation for the massive handshape spreading which seems to occur in ASL signs. Her model further suggests that holds are not present in the underlying structure of ASL signs, but may occur phonetically (list rhythm), phonologically (at utterance boundaries), morphologically (aspectual inflections on ASL verbs insert holds), and pragmatically (at the ends of conversational turns) (Wilbur 1987).

Wilbur (1982, 1990) has argued for a model of ASL phonology which incorporates syllables. In an early presentation of her model, Wilbur (1982) used a hierarchical model of syllable structure based on the work of Cairns and Feinstein (1982). A later model (Figure 3) incorporated Liddell's hold and movement segments (Wilbur 1990). In addition, Wilbur (1987) has explored the possible relations of the alternative model proposed by Sandler to a syllable structure of ASL.

Finally, Wilbur (1987) has insightfully brought out the relation between location (holds or target positions) and movement. She points out that path movement (as opposed to hand internal movement such as handshape change, flutter, wrist movement, and elbow rotation) is really a change in location. Thus, location and path movement are in direct opposition to each other because one is the dynamic counterpart of the other. Similar oppositions can be noted for handshape and orientation. Handshape change can be analyzed as the dynamic counterpart of handshape; likewise, orientation changes such as wrist movement or elbow rotation can be analyzed as the dynamic counterpart of orientation.

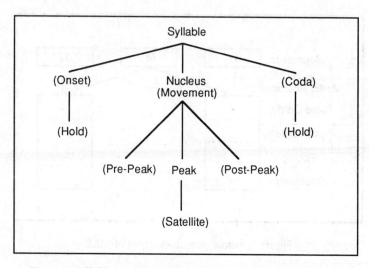

Figure 3. Syllable Model of ASL Phonology (from Wilbur, 1986)

Wilbur extends this analysis by noting that reduced dynamic forms also exist. For example, the tremored finger bend (flutter) used in the sign WHO can be analyzed as a reduced dynamic form of handshape change. Reduced dynamic forms also exist for location (tremored contact, as in KNOWLEDGE) and orientation (tremored wrist or elbow movement, as in LIGHT-YELLOW). Table 2 gives Wilbur's full analysis.

Table 2: Phonologically Related Static, Full Dynamic, and Reduced Dynamic Forms (from Wilbur, 1987)

Static	Full Dynamic	Reduced Dynamic
Handshape	Handshape change	Flutter/repeat bend
Location	Location change	Tremored contact
Orientation	Orientation change	Tremor (wrist/elbow)

Parallel to the work on ASL phonology has been research on the phonetic level of sign formation, particularly the search for distinctive features. Most of the work on this area has focussed on the handshape parameter.

In an early approach growing out of a study on sign diglossia, Woodward (1973a) defined 10 features which could be used to describe 40 handshapes. Woodward's distinctive feature system is given in Table 3.

Table 3: Woodward's (1973a) Handshape Distinctive Feature System

Distinctive feature	S	E	O	C	B	4	T	A	Á	B̈	B₂	5̈	5	ʊ	G	X	D	G₂	G̈	L
Closed	+	+	-	-	-	-	+	+	+	-	-	-	-	-	+	+	-	+	+	+
Thumb	-	-	-	-	-	-	-	+	+	+	+	+	+	+	-	-	-	+	+	+
Spread	-	-	-	-	-	+	-	-	+	-	-	-	+	+	-	-	-	-	-	+
Bent	-	-	-	+	-	+	-	+	-	-	+	-	+	-	+	-	-	-	+	-
Fore	-	-	-	+	+	+	+	-	-	+	+	+	+	+	+	+	+	+	+	+
Mid	-	-	-	+	+	+	-	-	-	+	+	+	+	-	-	-	-	-	-	-
Ring	-	-	-	+	+	+	-	-	-	+	+	+	+	+	-	-	-	-	-	-
Pinky	-	-	-	+	+	+	-	-	-	+	+	+	+	+	-	-	-	-	-	-
Contact	-	+	+	-	-	-	-	-	-	-	-	-	-	-	-	-	-	+	-	-
Crossed	-	-	-	-	-	-	+	-	-	-	-	-	-	-	-	-	-	-	-	-

Distinctive feature	I	Y	Ý	Ψ	7	8	H	N	V	R	3	K	M	W	6	F_N	9	F	M_t	N_t
Closed	+	+	+	-	-	-	+	+	+	+	+	+	+	+	-	+	-	+	+	+
Thumb	-	+	-	+	-	-	-	-	-	-	+	-	-	-	-	-	-	-	-	-
Spread	-	+	-	+	+	+	-	-	+	-	+	+	-	+	-	-	+	+	-	-
Bent	-	-	-	-	-	-	-	+	-	-	-	-	+	-	-	-	-	-	+	+
Fore	-	-	+	+	+	+	+	+	+	+	+	+	+	+	+	-	+	+	+	+
Mid	-	-	-	-	+	+	+	+	+	+	+	+	+	+	+	+	+	+	+	+
Ring	-	-	-	-	+	-	-	-	-	-	-	+	+	+	+	+	+	+	+	-
Pinky	+	+	+	+	+	+	-	-	-	-	-	-	-	-	-	+	+	+	-	+
Contact	-	-	-	-	+	+	-	-	-	-	-	-	-	+	+	+	+	+	-	-
Crossed	-	-	-	-	-	-	-	-	-	+	-	+	-	-	-	-	-	-	+	+

Lane, Boyes-Braem, and Bellugi (1976) described a distinctive feature system which was tested empirically by having deaf subjects view videotaped presentations of handshapes which had been masked electronically with visual noise. The results were analyzed using clustering techniques similar to those used in studies of spoken language phonetics. Their set of 11 distinctive features is described in Table 4.

Kegl and Wilbur (1976) used the Lane system to devise a set of distinctive features based on articulation, perception, and theoretical descriptive utility. Their system included two features, [extended] and [closed], to describe maximally opposed

Table 4: Lane, Boyes-Braem, and Bellugi's (1976) Distinctive Feature System

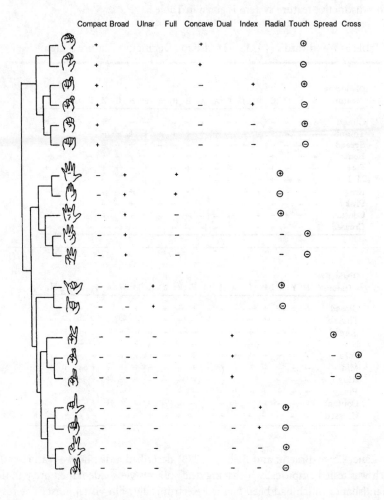

handshapes. Table 5 shows how these two features are used to describe a set of minimal feature specifications.

Finally, Mandel (1979, 1981) presented a detailed distinctive feature system including natural constraints imposed by anatomy in his discussion of phonotactics and morphophonology in ASL. An important concept introduced by Mandel was the grouping of handshapes based on selected and unselected fingers. The selected fin-

Table 5: Minimal Features Based on Kegl and Wilbur's
Distinctive Feature System (from Wilbur, 1987)

[+ extended, + closed]	G
[- extended, - closed]	O
[+ extended, - closed]	B
[- extended, + closed]	S

gers can be in any configuration, but they must all be in the same configuration. The unselected fingers may only be all extended or all closed. The grouping of hand-shapes by selected and unselected fingers serves to provide a foreground and background, or a figure and a ground, which Mandel suggested may facilitate perception and production.

In a psycholinguistic study of identification and discrimination of ASL hand-shapes, Stungis (1981) found that while binary models could be supported, a model in which handshape features varied continuously in two dimensions was more consistent with the data. The two-dimensional model proposed by Stungis used the features [extension] and [uniform breadth]. Defined in terms of production, as handshapes decrease in [extension] digits fold toward the palm of the hand; in perception, the perimeter of the image of the hand shrinks. Defined in terms of production, as handshapes decrease in [uniform breadth], motor commands to the five fingers are more various; in perception, the image of the hand appears less symmetrical about the middle finger.

Noting the similarity between this model of continuously variable visual distinctive features for handshape and models of acoustic distinctive features such as that of Repp (1977), Stungis (1981:273) concluded that "the same process of complex pattern recognition seems to extend across the linguistic experience of subjects and the sensory modality of stimuli."

Fingerspelling

Signs are only one means of representing meanings in the visual medium. Signed languages often incorporate a kind of manual alphabet called fingerspelling. Fingerspelling is often used for verbatim representation of English words, phrases, or sentences. It is also used to convey personal names, place names, names of months and holidays, and words for which no conventional signs yet exist such as technical English vocabulary. Fingerspelling is sometimes used to convey slang expressions

(N-O W-A-Y), and acronyms or other abbreviations (N-M 'New Mexico', N-M-A-D 'New Mexico Association of the Deaf').[3] People who closely follow English syntax in their signing may fingerspell certain English function words, such as prepositions (O-F), participles (B-E-E-N), and pronouns (H-E, S-H-E).

Fingerspelling can also be incorporated into an otherwise ASL utterance in a manner analogous to code-switching. Like the use of code-switching in spoken languages, this use of fingerspelling is often done for stylistic purposes. An example comes from a 1918 film of George Veditz, a deaf man, deaf educator, and President of the National Association of the Deaf. This film, "The Preservation of Sign Language," was made at a time when oralism was flourishing in Europe and just beginning to make an impact on American deaf education. Oralists condemned the use of signing in the education of deaf children. In the film, Veditz makes an impassioned plea for deaf people to preserve and protect their signed language. Speaking of oralists, he says, in quite eloquent ASL, "A new race of Pharaohs that knew not Joseph is taking over the land and many of our schools. They say that signing is worthless and of no help in the education of the deaf." Next, entirely in fingerspelling, he proclaims, "Enemies of sign language, they are enemies of the true welfare of the deaf." The impact which results both from the juxtaposition of ASL and English, and the stylistic device of fingerspelling the entire sentence, is dramatic.

Fingerspelling systems differ by country and by the signed language with which they are associated (Van Cleve, 1987). The American manual alphabet (Figure 4) uses a one-hand system historically related to a manual alphabet used in 17th century Spain. Great Britain uses a two-hand fingerspelling system unrelated to these systems. In Denmark, in addition to fingerspelling, the more frequently used Mouth-Hand System is based on syllabic representations of spoken Danish (Padden and LeMaster, 1985; Van Cleve, 1987). There are also systems for representing non-alphabetic symbols such as hand representations of Chinese characters.

A discussion of fingerspelling again raises the issue of languages and modalities for representing languages. Recall that there are three primary modalities: spoken, written, and signed. In order to understand the complex relations among languages and modes, it is instructive to look at how languages which are primarily associated with one modality can be represented in another modality.

If one were to ask what design questions need to be considered if one wanted to represent a spoken language in the written modality, the answer might take the form of Table 6.

The first design question that must be considered is, "What will be represented in writing?" A possible answer to this question is that words will be represented. One language that answers the design question this way is Chinese. Another possibility is to represent syllables in written form; Japanese opts for this solution. Finally, sounds

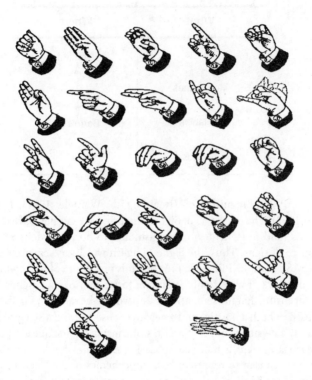

Figure 4. American Manual Alphabet (from Stokoe et al., 1965)

may be represented; English, as well as the many other languages that use alphabetic writing, has chosen this method. The second design question concerns the origin of the written marks. A range of solutions is possible, from outright invention of new "marks" — orthographies — to borrowing existing systems.[4]

The same design questions can be applied to the question of how a spoken language such as English can be represented in the signed modality (see Maxwell, 1990 for further discussion on the design of signed representations of spoken languages). The only difference relates to the second design question: the "marks" in this case are signs. Generically, these systems of representing English in the signed modality are called manual codes for English or Manually Coded English (MCE). Some typical solutions to this design problem are Signed English (Bornstein et al., 1973), Seeing Essential English (Anthony, 1971), Signing Exact English (Gustason, Pfetzing, and

Table 6: Design Features

What	Where
Words	Invented
Morphemes	↑
Syllables	↓ Borrowed
Sounds	

Zawolkow, 1972), Linguistics of Visual English (Wampler 1971), and Cued Speech (Cornett 1967). The inventors of Signed English, for example, have chosen to represent words (and morphemes) of English, and to borrow extensively from ASL as their source of signs. Thus, the Signed English word for "experience" is borrowed from the ASL word EXPERIENCE. While this procedure of borrowing heavily from ASL for the stock of signs results in similar forms for ASL and Signed English words, it does not ensure that the semantics of the two are the same. In English, "experience" can be used in both a positive and a negative sense, but the ASL word EXPERIENCE carries only a negative connotation. In some instances, the question of where to obtain the stock of signs is more complex. For example, the developers of the Signed English have chosen to represent both morphemes of the English word "development" in Signed English. ASL can be used as the source of the morpheme "develop", but there is no single morpheme in ASL which can be easily appropriated to represent the English morpheme "-ment".[5] Therefore, a sign for the morpheme "-ment" had to be devised.

The same design questions can be used to understand how a writing system for ASL could be developed. Although many systems have been proposed, none have become established within the deaf community. Some were attempts at developing phonetic transcription systems (Stokoe et al., 1965; Liddell and Johnson, 1986). A more recent approach (McIntire et al., 1987) attempts to develop a true phonemic writing system.

Placed in this framework, fingerspelling is distinctive because it is a tertiary system. That is, fingerspelling is a signed representation of written English, which is itself an alphabetic solution to the representation of a spoken language. As will be shown, many models of fingerspelling stop at this simple, historical/functional characterization. An important point to keep in mind, though, is that while this accurately describes the origins of fingerspelling, it does not provide an adequate characterization of how fingerspelling is learned by deaf children who are also acquiring ASL as their native language, how deaf or hearing adults perceive fingerspelling, or how fingerspelling production is organized as a skilled motor activity.

Lexical Borrowing

Lexical borrowing is a process in which words from one language are incorporated into another language, typically with extensive restructuring to make the foreign word more closely resemble the form of a native-language word. Along with this phonological restructuring, the semantics of the borrowed word is often modified, so that the resulting word has either a more limited or a wider scope of meaning (Burling, 1970; Fromkin and Rodman, 1974; Hudson, 1980).

An extensive discussion of lexical borrowing in ASL as been given by Battison (1978). Battison demonstrates that fingerspelled English words often become ASL signs in a process which he compares to lexical borrowing in spoken languages. When this happens, the fingerspelled word is restructured according to the phonological processes at work in ASL. Frequently, the semantics of the resulting loan sign are also different than the original, English word. A few ASL loan signs are given in Table 7.

Table 7: American Sign Language Loan Signs[6]

Loan Sign	English Origin	Meaning
#DO-DO	do	"What's happening?"
#ALL (a)	all	"All things on a list"
#ALL (b)	all	"Always" (durative)
#SO	so	"So what?" (sarcastically)

It is important to note that at the time Battison was writing, the prevailing conception of ASL phonology was still that signs were simultaneously organized. Fingerspelling, since it is a representation of written English letters, is sequential. Thus, the phonological restructuring of fingerspelled words as they are assimilated into ASL was seen as a process which maps a sequential underlying structure onto a simultaneous one. The precise nature of this sequential-to-simultaneous mapping was never adequately explored. In light of what is now known of ASL phonology, a critical re-analysis of the loan sign data is in order. Such a re-analysis might begin by examining how the sequences of fingerspelling are mapped onto the sequences of sign segments (e.g., Movements and Holds) during lexical borrowing. For example, it seems that the fingerspelled word A-L-L becomes a three segment (HMH) loan sign when it is incorporated into ASL as the loan sign #ALL.[6] The "A" fingerspelling handshape is associated with the initial H segment; the "L" fingerspelling handshape is associated with the final H segment. Autosegmental feature spreading would account for the featural details of the opening gesture associated with the M segment. Figure 5 shows this analysis using the diagrammatic conventions employed by Liddell.

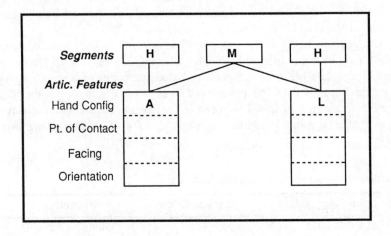

Figure 5. Autosegmental Analysis of the Loan Sign #ALL

Research on Fingerspelling

The lack of a satisfactory exploration of the sequential-to-simultaneous mapping process in lexical borrowing which was discussed above is indicative of a widespread assumption in the field of ASL linguistics that the study of fingerspelled words has little to tell us about the structure of signed words. Until the recent studies of sequentiality in ASL phonology, all indications were that signed words differed vastly from fingerspelled words (and spoken words) in their organization. It now seems that signed words, spoken words, and fingerspelled words may have a much more similar structure than was previously thought. An understanding of the structure of finger-spelling can indeed offer insights into the phonological structure of signed language

It is natural to consider signing and fingerspelling as similar: they are both examples of producing language in the signed modality. The same is not true, however, for fingerspelling and speaking. Even though both systems are sequentially organized, fingerspelling seems quite different from speech. First of all, fingerspelling and speech differ in modality. Moreover, as we have seen, fingerspelling is a tertiary system, a signed representation of written language.

It is possible, as the studies to be reported in later chapters will demonstrate, to apply concepts and techniques derived from recent investigations of speech to the study of fingerspelling. In short, the articulatory phonetics of fingerspelling and of speech can be studied in terms of kinematic and temporal variables common to both.

Fingerspelling as a Research Tool

ASL researchers typically make only passing reference to fingerspelling. Some researchers have used fingerspelling as a research tool to study, for example, language perception or deaf children's reading. Few of these investigations directly examined the phonetic or phonological structure of fingerspelling. Nevertheless, some information about the structure of fingerspelling can be gleaned from such studies.

Zakia and Haber (1971) report a study which examines the processing of sequential letter and word recognition in deaf and hearing subjects. Two significant pieces of information can be derived from their study. First, they found that the normal rate for fingerspelling words to a proficient reader was about 200 milliseconds per letter (1971:111). Second, their results suggest that:

> In reading fingerspelled words a highly experienced reader is not attending to the individual letters, but rather the total pattern of the finger configuration, or at least enough of that pattern to identify the word. Fingerspelling teachers recognize that those persons who attempt to form a word by identifying each letter of a word never gain proficiency in reading fingerspelling (1971:114).

Richards and Hanson (1985) conducted a study designed to examine the visual (perceptual) and production similarity of the 26 letters of the American manual alphabet. Forty deaf college students were asked to judge handshape similarity on either visual characteristics or aspects of manual shape production. Results indicated that visual and production similarity for the handshapes were essentially the same.

In a study by Locke and Locke (1971), deaf and hearing children were asked to recall lists of letters paired on the basis of phonetic (acoustic), visual, or dactylic similarity in an attempt to discern their coding strategies. Results showed that hearing children tended to code phonetically, while deaf children with unintelligible speech seemed to code dactylically.

Finally, Hanson, Liberman, and Shankweiler (1984) reported a study which found that deaf children who were classified as good readers used both speech and fingerspelling codes in short-term retention of printed letters, while deaf children classified as poor readers did not show influence of either of these linguistically based codes in recall. Thus, although the children's language system (in this case, English) was accessed by different modalities, signed versus spoken, both seemed to facilitate reading success.

Models of Fingerspelling

Most discussions of fingerspelling rely on a model which characterizes fingerspelling as a simple correspondence of handshapes with the printed letters of English words. According to this model, the production of fingerspelling consists of the serial transmission of static handshapes. Although fingerspelling unquestionably functions at some level in this fashion, the model is wholly inadequate for understanding how fingerspelling is acquired and fluently produced and perceived. In actual use, fingerspelling is presented in rapid and fluid succession. With the possible exceptions of the beginnings and endings of words, there seems to be no point at which the hand is fully static. The overall effect of fingerspelling is a smooth flow from one handshape to another, resulting not in a series of discrete signals but in one continuous signal. The individual handshapes in this signal influence each other in a way analogous to the way that the sounds which comprise a spoken word affect each other.

Klima and Bellugi's (1979:38) description of fingerspelling touches not only on the inadequacies of a simple model of fingerspelling, but also on the relation between the phonological structures of fingerspelling and signed languages.

> An internal organization of lexical units like that in spoken languages — basically sequential segments constituting lexical forms — is possible in the visual-gestural mode and in fact exists in systems of fingerspelling. In the American manual alphabet, for instance, the letters of English words are represented by distinct configurations of the hand, and meaningful units (English words as represented by their letters) are conveyed by sequences of these configurations. The fingerspelled word D-E-C-I-D-E, for instance, is composed of six configurations of the hand in sequence. In the hands of a

proficient signer they are produced rapidly, presenting a continuous signal and influencing each other in production — as do the sounds that make up a spoken word. Thus, though a fingerspelled word is realized as an uninterrupted flow (the signal), like a spoken word it has as its underlying structure a sequence of discrete elements. But fingerspelling is a derived, secondary gestural system, based on English.

Klima and Bellugi recognize that the rudimentary description of fingerspelling as "distinct configurations of the hand" representing an underlying structure of discrete elements must be refined in order to accurately model the structure of fingerspelling as it is actually produced. They do not, however, attempt to go beyond this rudimentary description. In addition, Klima and Bellugi place their discussion of fingerspelling within the context of the issue of sequentiality versus simultaneity in signed languages. Their conclusion is that since fingerspelling is sequentially produced and signs are primarily simultaneously produced, the study of fingerspelling holds little promise of contributing to our understanding of sign structure. Finally, Klima and Bellugi relegate fingerspelling to a secondary gestural system based on English. Bornstein (1978:338) expresses much the same view of fingerspelling.

> Technically, the manual alphabet is not a Sign system. It is really a variant of English print. Nevertheless, any reasonable degree of skill requires one to function at a word rather than a letter level. To read at a comfortable rate of transmission one must be able to see words and sometimes brief phrases. When sending, there is usually no conscious awareness of the individual letters.

Although Bornstein acknowledges that skilled performance of expressive and receptive fingerspelling requires the user to operate at a word level, he does not consider that a more linguistically sophisticated model of fingerspelling than "a variant of English print" would further our understanding of fingerspelling production and comprehension. Likewise, Tweney (1978:100) stops short of providing an adequate model of fingerspelling in his claim that "sign systems differ markedly from fingerspelled encodings of vocal languages, in which an alphabet is represented by hand gestures.... Such systems are not sign languages but, rather, manual encodings of vocal languages." Leaving aside the ambiguity of the term "sign languages" — fingerspelling is, indeed, a signed language — Tweney is undoubtedly correct in saying that fingerspelling (indirectly) represents a vocal language. The point is insufficient, however, since it tells us very little about how fluent fingerspelling is phonetically structured, produced as a coordinated motor skill, and fluently perceived.

Like Bloomfield's (1933:21) characterization of writing as a secondary system for representing spoken English, the net effect of these views of fingerspelling has been to draw attention away from what was considered the linguistically less important derived system in favor of studying the primary system. The result has been that in comparison to ASL, fingerspelling — its phonetic and phonological structure, acquisition, production, and perception — has received little attention from ASL linguists and psycholinguists.

A notable exception is the work of Akamatsu (1982, 1985). Akamatsu notes that the traditional, cipher model of fingerspelling, in which one hand configuration is associated with each letter of the alphabet, is inadequate to describe actual fingerspelling usage and acquisition data. She proposes an alternative model in which a *movement envelope* encloses the space in which a word is fingerspelled. The shape of the envelope at any given moment is determined by the hand configuration being produced; changes in hand configuration cause the envelope to expand, contract, or otherwise change shape. Movement envelopes for various fingerspelled words are shown in Figure 6.

Akamatsu found support for the movement envelope model from deaf children's acquisition of fingerspelling. She grouped a corpus of data from children aged 3;8 to 5;2 into three types: imitations, spontaneous utterances with clear hand configurations, and spontaneous utterances with unintelligible hand configurations. The children's imitations, although inaccurate compared to adult forms, retained a general gestalt of the fingerspelled word. Akamatsu states that (1985:128):

> the HCs [hand configurations] differ, but the gross opening and closing movements of the hand are preserved. Initial and final HC segments are likely to be copied correctly.

Spontaneous utterances containing clear hand configurations preserved not individual hand configurations but whole words as represented by their envelopes. The resulting fingerspelled words often did not resemble English words (Figure 6). The final type of utterance could be understood as words even though the individual hand configurations were not clear. These words were similar to the second type of word except that the children fingerspelled the entire word very rapidly.

Akamatsu's work is an important advance over the traditional, cipher model of fingerspelling. In its present formulation, however, her movement envelope model offers only a limited discussion of the kinematic and temporal details of fingerspelling movement. The next questions are: In production, how do signers put letters into envelopes; in perception, how do receivers extract letters from envelopes?

Target   **Child**

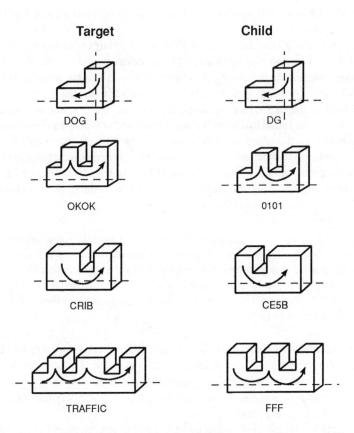

Figure 6. Movement Envelopes (from Akamatsu, 1985)

The Production and Perception of Fingerspelling

The nature of the models that are used to characterize fingerspelling is important in many ways. One way is the predictions that the models make about the production and perception of fingerspelling.

A simple, cipher model of fingerspelling, for example, represents fingerspelling as the serial transmission of static handshapes corresponding in both the producer's and the receiver's conception to the printed letters of the English alphabet. This model makes no prediction regarding the shape of the resulting movement envelope, nor the existence of transitions between handshapes. According to this model, the total production and perceptual content of a fingerspelled word is the sum of the individual letters.

Alternatively, a model of fingerspelling which incorporates movement envelopes as does Akamatsu's, and which recognizes the dynamic character of actual fingerspelling, suggests that learning to fingerspell would involve learning both the static hand configurations and the set of possible transitions. Such a model would further predict that in production and perception, the significant organizing unit is likely to be not the individual letter but some more abstract unit which incorporates both handshapes (locations or targets) and the transitional movements between them. According to this model, the total production and perceptual content of a fingerspelled word is more than the sum of the individual letters Padden and LeMaster (1985:168) explicitly adopt the assumptions of such a model in their study of deaf children's acquisition of fingerspelling.

> When learning to fingerspell, the young child needs to master several sets of skills. First, each of the 26 hand configurations must be mastered. The characteristic positioning of the hand in a fixed central location for executing the sequence of handshapes must also be learned. And finally, the child needs to learn the set of possible transition movements from one hand configuration to the next.

Moreover, such a model predicts that deaf children's early production of fingerspelling will not be organized in terms of letters, but in terms of complex, wholistic movements which are only later differentiated into individual letters. As will be shown in the next section, this is precisely what is found in deaf children's acquisition of fingerspelling.

A study by Hanson (1981) directly addresses the perception of fingerspelling as whole words versus individual letters. Sixty fingerspelled words were presented to skilled deaf signers of American Sign Language. Half were real words ranging in length from five to thirteen letters. These words were matched by length with 30 nonwords. Twenty of these were pseudowords such as BRANDIGAN and CADERMELTON; two were impossible English words such as FTERNAPS and VETMFTERN.

Hanson asked her subjects to view and recall the stimulus items. Analysis of the results indicated a difference in ability to receive and report words, pseudowords, and non-words. These results suggested that "words and pseudowords were not processed as individual letters. Rather, processing of a given letter was influenced by other letters of the item" (Hanson 1981:178). Impossible words, on the other hand, did seem to be processed as individual letters.

One factor influencing the perception of fingerspelling may be speed, although little empirical data are available on fingerspelling speed. As noted previously, Zakia and Haber (1971) reported an average rate of 200 milliseconds per letter. Bornstein (1965) reported that the natural fingerspelling rate for ASL signers is about 354 letters per minute, or 169 milliseconds per letter. In Hanson's (1981) study of fingerspelling perception, her stimulus materials were produced by a deaf native ASL signer at an average rate of 369 letters per minute (163 milliseconds per letter) for words and 339 letters per minute (177 milliseconds per letter) for non-words. Battison (1978) reported a typical rate of 6 letters per second (167 milliseconds per letter).

It seems clear, however, that more than speed is involved in the proficient production and reception of fingerspelling. Akamatsu (1982) noted, for example, that when adult deaf signers are asked how to learn to comprehend fingerspelling, they emphasize paying attention to the shape of the entire word. Akamatsu reported that fingerspelling by deaf adults is often unintelligible when broken down into individual segments, yet perfectly intelligible when taken as a whole. A concern with shape, movement envelopes, whole words, or some other unit which is "more than the sum of its parts" is widespread in the literature on fingerspelling production and perception.

Learning to Fingerspell

These considerations about the production and perception of fingerspelling become critical for understanding the acquisition of fingerspelling by deaf children and hearing adults.

Researchers are only now beginning to study children's acquisition of fingerspelling. What little evidence is currently available about the acquisition of fingerspelling suggests that children initially conceive of fingerspelled words as complex signs. Only later do these two types of "signs" — fingerspelled words and actual signs — diverge into two distinct systems in the child's grammar. As we have seen, Akamatsu (1985) called this complex "sign" a movement envelope. She goes on to note that children reproduce the gross features of the envelope before they recognize the individual letters. Akamatsu describes a stunning example of this (1985:131). A deaf native signer reported that when he was a child, his mother did the grocery shopping at a Safeway store. As a child, he saw his mother fingerspell "Safeway" often and could produce a gestalt of the word; in Akamatsu' model, he was producing a movement envelope (Figure 7). One day, when he was about nine years old, he realized that this word could be broken down into the English words SAFE and WAY. When he tried fingerspelling it, he realized that the hand configuration pattern that his mother had been using was in fact S-A-F-E-W-A-Y, and that he had been producing

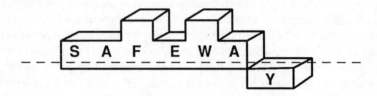

Figure 7. Movement Envelope for SAFEWAY (from Akamatsu, 1985)

an approximation of it for years. His perception and production of S-A-F-E-W-A-Y had for years been in terms of a form, a word, in which the internal structure referred not to individual English letters but to a movement pattern. This suggests a model of fingerspelling structure in which each fingerspelled word is a complex "sign". Like an ASL sign, the fingerspelled word will have an internal structure consisting of segments, but the segments will not correspond in the learner's grammar to English letters.

This view is supported in Padden and LeMaster's (1985) study of deaf children's acquisition of fingerspelling. Examining acquisition data collected from six deaf children at ages varying from 2;3 to 7;11, they found evidence to suggest that deaf children "construct a theory about how fingerspelling works in ways independent of English orthography and morphology" (1985:166). Attempts by young children to produce fingerspelling involved a sequence of at least three hand configurations. For example, when a young child was asked for her name, she fingerspelled E-U-B; when asked for her dog's name, she fingerspelled U-B-A. Often in early fingerspelling, only the initial letter was distinct; the following letters were not clearly articulated, but the overall form of the child's imitation closely resembled true fingerspelling.

Very little research has been devoted to hearing adult's second language acquisition of fingerspelling. Guillory (1966) was one of the first to recognize that the traditional model of fingerspelling as a simple handshape/letter correspondence was not conducive to effective second language learning of fingerspelling. As she noted (1966:1):

> An old and common approach to fingerspelling was that the interested hearing person obtained a manual alphabet card, from which he learned the twenty-six different hand positions that represent the letters of the alphabet. Then he set about spelling out words letter by letter. With constant practice

this person eventually learned to spell and see words, but, in many instances, others using this method continued to spell out each word and see only letters, never whole words, when reading fingerspelling.

A simple comparison of first- and second-language acquisition of fingerspelling is revealing. For children acquiring fingerspelling, the problem seems to be to learn that fingerspelling corresponds to English orthography. Their initial hypothesis is that fingerspelling is a complex "sign". It is only later in their development that children begin to conceptualize fingerspelling as a correspondence with English written letters. The problem is reversed for adult learners. They must try to forget that the units of fingerspelling correspond to individual letters and must learn instead to perceive fingerspelling as whole words. Guillory's approach was to present students with fingerspelled representations of common English phonetic combinations, such as A-B, A-S, I-M, Q-U-E, and so forth in rapid and repetitive drills until the students learned to see these sequences as holistic gestures. This approach is still one of the most popular methods for teaching adults how to fingerspell. Variations of Guillory's approach form the basis for many fingerspelling activities currently used in second-language classrooms (Mowl, 1983).

Fingerspelling Fluency

No research exists examining fingerspelling fluency. The production of fingerspelling is usually described only in subjective, anecdotal terms, and even then only the grossest features receive attention. For example, signed language and interpreter educators often speak of "staccato" or "jerky" fingerspelling; fingerspelling can also be produced too smoothly, with not enough definition between the letters. A common misconception among fingerspelling students is that fluency correlates with speed. This is certainly not the case, and often leads students to develop poor fingerspelling skills. The relation between speed and fluency in fingerspelling is apparently quite complex.[7] Some native signers fingerspell rather slowly, yet we would surely judge them to be "fluent". Others may fingerspell quite rapidly, yet their production is fluent and easy to perceive.

Factors such as evenness or rhythmicity of movement and coordination among the individual articulators are likely to be important in the fluent production of fingerspelling. Until they are studied and described in precise and quantifiable ways, however, our understanding of what constitutes fluent fingerspelling will remain elementary.

Coarticulation in Fingerspelling

Daniloff and Hammarberg (1973:239) offer a concise definition of coarticulation:

> The notion of coarticulation presupposes the existence of segments, i.e.
> canonical forms of articulation. Coarticulation results from the interaction
> of these canonical segments by means of a mechanism ... which might in-
> volve "feature spreading", i.e. the spreading of a feature inherent to one ca-
> nonical segment to another segment to which the feature is not inherent.
> The result of this process is a "smoothing out" of the transitions between the
> segments and thus turns a sequence of entities into a continuum.

Daniloff and Hammarberg (1973) assume that these canonical targets are represented at some level as invariant, ideal forms. These targets serve as input to an articulation mechanism which is characterized by mechano-inertial, anatomical, and
neurological constraints. Articulatory movements are the output of this articulation
process.

Two types of coarticulation have been described: left-to-right or carry-over
coarticulation, and right-to-left or anticipatory coarticulation. The English word
'spoon' can be used to illustrate both types (Daniloff and Hammarberg, 1973). In
their canonical forms, /s/, /p/, and /n/ do not have lip-rounding; /u/ is specified for
lip-rounding. When the word 'spoon' is spoken, however, lip-rounding occurs in all
segments. Thus, anticipatory coarticulation occurs for the segments /s/ and /p/, while
carry-over coarticulation appears on the segment /n/.

Both types of coarticulation can appear in fingerspelling. For example, the fingerspelled letter A is not specified for movement; the fingerspelled letter Z is made
with a zigzag movement. When the word M-A-Z-E is fingerspelled, the movement
of the Z spreads into the A segment. Thus, anticipatory coarticulation of features associated with the letter Z is modifying the canonical form for the letter A. Likewise,
the fingerspelled letter H is a two-fingered handshape; E is canonically represented
as a four-fingered handshape (the four fingers resting on the thumb). In the fingerspelled word H-E, the letter E is often made as a two-fingered handshape. In this example, carry-over coarticulation from the featural specification of the letter H
modifies the articulation of the letter E.

Evidence for coarticulation in fingerspelling has been described only sparsely in
the literature on fingerspelling. For example, Richards and Hanson (1985:319) men-
tion in passing that "in skilled fingerspelling, letters of words are neither produced
nor recognized as isolated letters. Rather, one finds evidence for coarticulatory effects in production."

The most extensive discussion of coarticulation in fingerspelling appears in the work of Reich (Reich, 1975; Reich and Bick, 1976, 1977). Reich described several instances of the phonological restructuring of fingerspelling such as is found in carryover and anticipatory coarticulation. For example, Reich (1975) noted that 2-fingered and 4-fingered features can spread in both directions. The wrist twist (supination) of /g/ and /h/ also tends to affect both preceding and following letters. Other features were changed in one direction or another. For example, Reich describes forward assimilation (carry-over coarticulation) occurring with thumb-tuckedness, wrist-bentness, finger-outness, and finger-and-pinkie-togetherness.[8] Thumb-outness, finger-apartness, and thumb-pinky-togetherness appear to undergo backward assimilation (anticipatory coarticulation).

This line of research is important because it suggests that the same principles used to study the phonetics and phonology of sound-based languages can be brought to bear on the study of signed language. The issue of coarticulation makes it clear that the correspondence of handshapes with English print is not the most significant factor structuring fingerspelling. Notions of segmentation such as targets and transitions intrinsic to the phonological structure of fingerspelling must be developed and studied in fine phonetic detail. As Reich noted: "we find the same phenomena in fingerspelling that we find in the phonology of vocal speech" (1975:353).

Kinematics, Dynamics, and Articulatory Movements

"Motion may be defined as a continuous change of position" (Sears and Zemansky, 1949:51). *Kinematics* is the study of the motion of an object without regard to the forces acting on it; the study of motion which considers the forces which cause the object's motion is called *dynamics* (Meirovitch, 1985).

It should be noted that the word "dynamic" does not always refer to dynamics in this technical sense. Often, the term is used in a lay sense merely to mean that something is moving or changing. Previously, for example, it was noted that Wilbur (1987) characterized sign movement as static, reduced dynamic, and fully dynamic. Used in this sense, "dynamic" does not refer to dynamics — the study of motion in terms of the forces acting on a moving body — but to the fact that the handshape, location, or orientation of the sign is changing.

The two fields, kinematics and dynamics, are related in a way analogous to the distinction between phonetics and phonology (Kelso, 1986:109-110):

> What are the essential control structures that govern the patterning of articulator motion in space and time? Obviously there are many surface features of a movement that one might propose as significant candidates for

controlled variables. What then, fashions the constraints on the choices one makes? ... [D]ynamics can be viewed as the simplest and most abstract description of the motion of a system.... [K]inematics provides a surface description of the movements of a system which are generated from a given type of dynamical organization.

Kinematics describes the surface form of observed motion, while dynamics describes the underlying system which accounts for these observed motions. "Relations among kinematic variables are useful to describe the space-time behavior of articulators, but it is dynamics that cause such motions" (Kelso, Vatikiotis-Bateson, Saltzman, and Kay, 1985:275). Just as phonological structure must be inferred from phonetics, it is also possible "to infer the structure of the underlying dynamics from the kinematics of articulator motions during either discrete or rhythmic tasks" (ibid.).

Kinematics and dynamics can be readily related to speech by studying the motions of articulators. Early kinematic studies of speech used cineradiography to examine, for example, tongue movements (Kent, 1972; Kuehn and Moll, 1976); later techniques such as ultrasound were adapted to provide a look at speech movements (Parush, Ostry, and Munhall, 1983). Finally, Kelso and his associates have used sophisticated motion tracking techniques similar to those described in Chapter Three in several studies of speech articulatory movement (Kelso and Tuller, 1984; Kelso, Vatikiotis-Bateson, Saltzman and Kay, 1985; Kelso, Saltzman, and Tuller, 1986).

A dynamic approach to speech production is now beginning to emerge in speech research. This approach relies on equations used to describe nonlinear, harmonic motion similar to that of damped springs to model the forces at work in the production of speech (Browman and Goldstein, 1985; Kelso, Saltzman, and Tuller, 1986; Kelso and Tuller, 1984; Kugler, Kelso, and Turvey, 1982). This approach has also been extended into coordinated, non-linguistic movements (Kelso, Tuller, and Harris, 1983). The dynamic account of speech production assumes that dynamic variables such as tension and damping are controlled rather than kinematic variables such as distance or rate.

Finally, Poizner and his colleagues (Poizner, Bellugi, and Lutes-Driscoll, 1981; Poizner, 1983; Poizner, Newkirk, and Bellugi, 1983; Poizner, Klima, Bellugi, and Livingston, 1986) have conducted several series of studies which examined the kinematics of ASL movements.

Organization of the Studies

While our understanding of the phonetic and phonological structure of signed languages such as ASL continues to grow, we know very little about other types of signed languages such as fingerspelling. Based on this review of the literature, we can identify two areas for further research: acquisition of fingerspelling by adult, second language learners; and the phonetic structure of fingerspelling. The areas form the focus of the studies reported in later chapters.

Learning to Fingerspell

Adult, second language acquisition of signed languages has gone virtually unstudied by researchers. Until recently, acquisition of signed languages (with the exception of Manually Coded English systems) has proceeded only on an informal basis. With the growth of signed language classes in colleges and universities, and with the burgeoning number of interpreter training programs around the country, more and more adults are able to learn ASL and fingerspelling in a formal, classroom situation.

Prior assumptions about the ease or difficulty of the task faced by adults learning signed languages clearly are no longer sufficient. For many years, it was assumed that adequate instruction in fingerspelling consisted in nothing more than giving students a card indicating the twenty-six handshapes of the manual alphabet.

Much more empirical research is needed on the complex language learning situation faced by adults learning signed languages and especially fingerspelling. As a first step, the following question should be considered:

1. Which language-learning tasks do students consider the easiest and which are the most difficult? What can data about the relative ease or difficulty of learning to produce and comprehend signed languages and fingerspelling tell us about the structure of fingerspelling?

The Phonetics of Fingerspelling

Simple, cipher models of fingerspelling which characterize it only as a handshape-letter correspondence have been shown to be inadequate for understanding how fingerspelling is learned, either by deaf children or by hearing adults; how it is perceived and comprehended; and how it is fluently produced.

Models of fingerspelling such as Akamatsu's (1982, 1985) have done much to advance our understanding of the problems inherent in the production, perception, and comprehension of fingerspelling. What is now needed is detailed temporal and kinematic data taken from actual fingerspelling on which to build, test, and revise models of fingerspelling. Among the many questions which could be asked, the following seem especially crucial:

1. What are the characteristics of fingerspelled letters and the transitions between letters in fluent fingerspelling? What can kinematic and temporal information about fingerspelling targets and transitions tell us about the production and perception of fingerspelling?
2. How can the speed of fingerspelling be studied? What are typical speeds for fingerspelling?
3. What are the temporal and kinematic characteristics of fluent fingerspelling? What can we learn about the production and perception of fingerspelling by examining the production of fluent versus non-fluent fingerspelling?
4. Is there any evidence for a dynamic view of fingerspelling production?

The studies reported in the following chapters address the questions identified above. Chapter 2 describes a study which sought to determine whether hearing, adult college students feel that learning to produce and comprehend fingerspelling is easy or difficult compared to the other language-learning tasks which they face.

Chapters 4 and 5 describe studies of kinematic and temporal aspects of fingerspelling. These studies relied on techniques of three-dimensional motion tracking and analysis which are described in chapter 3.

Chapter 4 examines temporal characteristics of fingerspelling targets and transitions and presents the preliminaries of a dynamic view of fingerspelling production. Chapter 5 follows up on the discussion of dynamics started in chapter 4 by describing several kinematic and temporal aspects of fluent and non-fluent fingerspelling. The findings provide preliminary evidence that fingerspelling production can be insightfully understood within a dynamic framework. Finally, chapter 6 discusses the implications of these findings and presents suggestions for further research, offering conclusions concerning a unified view of signed and spoken languages as gestures.

Chapter 2
Learning to Fingerspell

Adult Acquisition of Fingerspelling

Although very little research exists on adult second language acquisition of finger-spelling, experience makes it clear that the task is extremely difficult. Students frequently express the opinion that learning to produce and comprehend fingerspelling is one of the most difficult tasks they face when learning a signed language. Professional signed language interpreters who are not native users of ASL and fingerspelling report that difficulties in understanding fingerspelling are a frequent source of problems. One reason why these problems are so serious is that fingerspelled words and phrases often contain critical information. Inability to comprehend one fingerspelled word or phrase can easily result in one missing the entire point of a conversation.

Students learning a second spoken language face a number of tasks. They must learn to speak the language and to comprehend the language when spoken by others. These others may be native or non-native users of that language. They typically must also learn to read and write in that language. Signed language students face several similar and a few different tasks. First of all, the language situation in the deaf community requires that students of signed languages learn three languages: ASL, manual codes for English (MCE), and Pidgin Sign English (PSE).[1] Signed language students have to acquire expressive and receptive proficiency in a language (ASL) different in structure than their native language and which is produced in another modality. They also must acquire proficiency in a pidgin language and a signed representation of their native language. Unlike the typical student of a second spoken language, however, signed language students do not need to learn to read and write another language, since ASL and PSE have no written forms. Fingerspelling and loan signs cut across the language issue, sometimes representing ASL (as in the case of loan signs) and other times English.

Similar to the native/non-native question is the issue of whether the person signing to the student is deaf or hearing. This factor often influences the linguistic and cultural background that the signer brings to the communicative setting and affects the nature of the communication presented to the student. In the case of fingerspelling, deaf signers who are native users of ASL may choose different lexical items to fingerspell than hearing or English dominant signers. This factor also affects the student's ability to receive the message. For many students, interacting with deaf, native signers is often accompanied by anxiety. If, as Krashen (1985) suggests, an affective filter is in operation whenever we attempt to understand or to produce a second language, then this factor could be quite important in learning to understand signed language and fingerspelling.

Most literature and textbooks dealing with second language acquisition of signed languages focus on teaching ASL and PSE. Programs which offer instruction in signed languages frequently spend most of their time and effort in developing skills in ASL or PSE. Although it is widely accepted that skill in fingerspelling is critical, it is often the weakest component in the signed language curriculum.

One reason for this may be the paucity of research on the structure of fingerspelling. Battison's (1978) work on lexical borrowing, for example, can be used to develop learning activities for teaching students how to produce and comprehend loan signs. Without any research on the production and comprehension of fingerspelling, however, instructors are forced to discuss fingerspelling in only the most subjective manner.

Another factor may also be involved. It is generally accepted by teachers that one of the most difficult tasks faced by signed language students is to produce native-like ASL. It must be noted, however, that many instructors had deaf parents from whom they learned signed language and fingerspelling informally as children. Even instructors who learned as adult, second language learners usually did so in situations quite different from those faced by the current college- level signed language student. The modern signed language curriculum, with its separation of language instruction into ASL, PSE, MCE, and fingerspelling modules, is a relatively recent phenomenon. We simply do not understand the enormity of the task faced by signed language students. A reasonable first step would be to ask the students what they feel is the relative ease or difficulty associated with the various learning tasks in the signed language classroom.

Method

Subjects

Thirty college students enrolled in signed language courses at the University of New Mexico took part in this study. All subjects had completed enough signed language courses to provide them with sufficient background to be able to rate the relative difficulties of various learning activities associated with the signed language classroom.

Materials

Twelve activities associated with learning signed languages and fingerspelling were identified. These activities cut across the three broad factors discussed above: language (ASL, MCE, PSE, or fingerspelling); comprehension versus production; and, in the case of comprehension, whether the signer is hearing or deaf. The twelve activities listed in Table 8 were used as items on a survey.

Procedures

Subjects were given a survey packet with a cover sheet describing the procedures to be followed and a rating form. They were told that the survey was designed to determine which activities related to learning signed languages students found to be most difficult, and which they found easiest. The subjects were not given any indication that the experimenter was primarily interested in fingerspelling. They were instructed to rank the activities from 1 to 12, with 1 being easiest and 12 hardest. Subjects were instructed to rank the activities in terms of their intrinsic ease or difficulty and not to associate activities with individual teachers or specific classes.

Results

The item rankings were analyzed in terms of their medians and standard deviations. Table 9 provides descriptive statistics for the 12 activities. Figure 8 displays the individual item means and standard deviations. Activity 2, "understanding fingerspelling when produced by a deaf person", was consistently ranked the most difficult. The next most difficult activity was Activity 6, "understanding ASL when

Table 8: Signed Language Learning Activities

No.	Activity	Label
1.	Understanding Pidgin Sign English when produced by a hearing signer.	U-PSE-H
2.	Understanding fingerspelling when produced by a deaf person.	U-FS-D
3.	Producing American Sign Language.	P-ASL
4.	Understanding Manually Coded English when produced by a deaf person.	U-MCE-D
5.	Producing fingerspelling.	P-FS
6.	Understanding American Sign Language when produced by a deaf person.	U-ASL-D
7.	Producing Pidgin Sign English.	P-PSE
8.	Understanding American Sign Language when produced by a hearing person.	U-ASL-H
9.	Understanding fingerspelling when produced by a hearing person.	U-FS-H
10	Producing Manually Coded English (any system).	P-MCE
11.	Understanding Pidgin Sign English when produced by a deaf person.	U-PSE-D
12.	Understanding Manually Coded English when produced by a hearing person.	U-MCE-H

produced by a deaf person." These two activities were compared by means of a paired sample t-test to determine if the difference in ranking was significant. The results (Table 10) indicate that Activity 2 was ranked significantly more difficult than Activity 6: $t = 2.63$, $p < .01$ (one-tail).

Discussion

Students overwhelmingly feel that learning to understand fingerspelling, especially when produced by a deaf person, is the most difficult challenge that they face, even more difficult that what is generally thought to be the most difficult task in a signed language classroom, learning to produce ASL. In fact, the subjects felt that several activities were more difficult than this task. Understanding ASL when produced by a deaf person was rated the second most difficult learning activity, but not as difficult

Table 9: Descriptive Statistics For Learning Activities

Activity[a]	Mean	Std. Dev	Minimum	Maximum	N	Label
1(10)	4.23	2.62	1.00	11.00	30	U-PSE-H
2(1)	10.70	2.15	4.00	12.00	30	U-FS-D
3(6)	7.23	3.35	1.00	12.00	30	P-ASL
4(5)	7.53	2.18	4.00	11.00	30	U-MCE-D
5(11)	3.50	2.46	1.00	10.00	30	P-FS
6(2)	9.23	3.29	1.00	12.00	30	U-ASL-D
7(12)	2.30	2.02	1.00	10.00	30	P-PSE
8(4)	7.80	2.48	3.00	11.00	30	U-ASL-H
9(3)	8.27	2.07	4.00	11.00	30	U-FS-H
10(9)	4.97	3.01	1.00	12.00	30	P-MCE
11(7)	6.27	2.16	2.00	10.00	30	U-PSE-D
12(8)	6.07	2.60	1.00	12.00	30	U-MCE-H

a. The number in parentheses is the rank order of the item, from most difficult (1) to least difficult (12).

as understanding fingerspelling when produced by a deaf person. Producing ASL was ranked sixth in order of difficulty, after understanding fingerspelling, ASL, and even after understanding MCE when produced by a deaf person.

These results indicate which activities students of signed languages find difficult. A comparison of which learning tasks are grouped together can provide valuable information about the nature of these tasks. The original identification of tasks used three categories: language, production/reception, and status of signer. Several questions arise concerning the nature of these categories. Based on the difficulty of learning signed languages, should we group languages regardless of production/reception, or should we group together production/reception in the signed modality regardless of language? In the first instance, for example, producing and understanding ASL would form a separate category from producing and understanding MCE. In the second instance, producing ASL and MCE would form a distinct task from understanding ASL and MCE.

A second question concerns the categorization of fingerspelling. Where should fingerspelling be grouped? A plausible answer would be that fingerspelling is the manual representation of English letters, and thus should be grouped with MCE

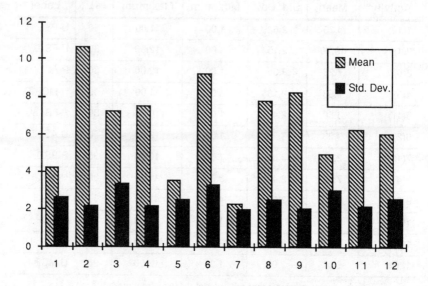

Figure 8. Learning Activity Rankings

Table 10: t-Test Results, Activities Two and Six.

Variable	Number of Cases	Mean	Standard Deviation	Standard Error
Activity 2	30	10.73	2.152	.393
Activity 6	30	9.23	3.287	.600

t Value	Degrees of Freedom	2-Tail Probability
2.63	29	.014

rather than with ASL.[2] This impression may not be borne out when production and processing factors, such as would affect the ease or difficulty of learning, are taken into consideration.

rather than with ASL.[2] This impression may not be borne out when production and processing factors, such as would affect the ease or difficulty of learning, are taken into consideration.

Cluster analysis provides one way of exploring these questions. The data from the survey were used as input into a cluster analysis.[3] The results are displayed as a dendrogram, which shows the hierarchy of the clusters being combined (Figure 9).

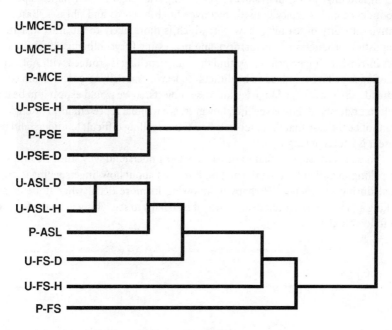

Figure 9. Dendrogram

The results of the cluster analysis highlight several interesting relationships. Each cluster can be identified on the dendrogram in Figure 9. The first cluster identified includes Activities 4 and 12, understanding MCE. The second cluster identified includes Activities 6 and 8, understanding ASL. A three-cluster analysis identifies the following groups: (1) understanding and producing MCE; (2) understanding and producing PSE, and (3) understanding and producing ASL. Considered in terms of relative difficulty of learning, the activities seem to fall into groups identified by languages and not by reception or production.

Fingerspelling (understanding fingerspelling when produced by a deaf person) appears at the fourth level and is grouped with ASL. Producing fingerspelling clusters at a still later level and again falls into the ASL group. At the topmost level, understanding and producing MCE and PSE are combined into one group (Activities 4, 12, 10, 1, 7, and 11), and understanding and producing ASL and fingerspelling are combined into another (Activities 6, 8, 3, 2, 9, and 5).

Based on historical or functional relationships, we might be led to group fingerspelling and English together, since fingerspelling is an English letter/handshape correspondence and is typically used to convey English words and phrases. Based on relative difficulty of learning, however, which is more likely to tap into structural (linguistic), production (articulatory), and processing (psycholinguistic) characteristics intrinsic to fingerspelling, we find that fingerspelling is grouped with ASL. Like ASL, fingerspelling is judged to be difficult to learn, especially to perceive and comprehend. ASL is a foreign language for these subjects, so we would expect it to be difficult to understand. Fingerspelling, however, is a manual representation of English; it cannot be the case that these subjects find fingerspelling difficult to understand because it is a foreign language.

These results suggest that in order to better understand why students find fingerspelling so difficult more information is needed about how fingerspelling is organized during production. Perhaps by knowing in more detail what students are looking at, we can better understand why it is so hard to see. This will be the focus of the following chapters.

Chapter 3
The Measurement of
Fingerspelling Movement

Background

Phonetics has a long history of studying the movements of vocal tract articulators; no kinematic or dynamic studies of fingerspelling articulatory movements have been undertaken. The studies to be reported in chapters four and five were designed to address this deficiency by examining several kinematic and temporal features of fingerspelling. The present chapter provides a broad overview of the equipment and techniques used in these studies. First, the hardware and software used are described and a sample data analysis of one data-file is provided. Finally, the procedures used in the studies which are reported in the following chapters are described.

Hardware

The production of fingerspelling and loan signs involves rapid, complex movements of small articulators in three-dimensional space. The speed and complexity of these movements place several requirements on the equipment used in their study. The equipment must be able to make precise measurements of fine movements in three dimensions. The sampling rate must be high enough to capture the rapidly changing articulators. A standard videotape, with a sampling rate of 30 frames/second or 60 fields/second, does not meet this requirement. The equipment must also provide a way to analyze and display the data. Again, videotape does not meet this requirement, since it does not provide an efficient way of converting images into kinematic data. Finally, the equipment must be non-intrusive. Certain equipment, such as the accelerometers used in biomechanics research, restrain the movements of the subject to such an extent that very fine or complex motions cannot be studied.

Movement data were collected with a piece of equipment called the Waterloo Spatial Motion Analysis and Recording Technique (WATSMART). WATSMART is a non-contact, three-dimensional digitizing system. It is capable of recording high velocity kinematic motion as well as high resolution displacements.

The WATSMART system configuration used in this study consisted of four basic components: a set of infrared, light-emitting diode (IRED) markers; two infrared sensitive cameras; a chassis containing the WATSMART electronics; and an IBM-AT microcomputer equipped with a 30 megabyte hard disk and 640K of RAM, used to control the system, to buffer incoming data, and to store the raw data-files.

Data acquisition with WATSMART requires the attachment of small, infrared light-emitting diode markers to the articulators which are to be monitored for movement. These markers emit light in a more than 140-degree cone. Markers are attached to the subject and then connected to a controller by approximately six feet of 32-gauge shielded wire. The controllers are 83 millimeters long, 35 millimeters wide, and 9.5 millimeters thick; they weigh 1.2 ounces. The controllers serve as a power source for the IREDs and also control the pulsing of individual IREDs. Each controller can accommodate up to 8 markers; in this study only three markers were used, and thus only one controller was needed. The controller is connected to the WATS-MART chassis by a length of 26-gauge, telephone wire.

Each marker is strobed in sequence for a period of 65 microseconds by the controller. Thus, only one marker is actually active at any point in time. As the subject moves, the instantaneous position of each marker is digitized at aggregate rates up to 4700 Hz.

Movement of the IREDs is detected by two infrared sensitive cameras. Each camera has a 33 degree by 33 degree square field of view and can detect markers from 1.1 to 10 meters away without any focus adjustment. The standard field coverage is 1.2 meters of width and height for every 2 meters of distance between camera and marker. Figure 10 shows the field of view for a camera.

Each camera lens focuses an image of the IRED marker onto a two-dimensional photosensitive sensor. The resulting signals are amplified, converted to twelve bit digital values by the circuitry inside the camera, and transmitted to the camera system controller board in the system chassis. The values are then transformed into two-dimensional coordinates which are relayed to the host computer for storage. Data is first buffered to the computer's RAM in order to allow for high acquisition rates. At the end of each data-collection trial, the data are stored on the computer's hard disk. Trial length in seconds must be taken into consideration since there must be enough memory on the host computer to buffer the complete trial. Each camera requires four bytes per marker per frame (the number of frames is determined by the sampling rate) to buffer data. Using the present study as a guide, a trial would require

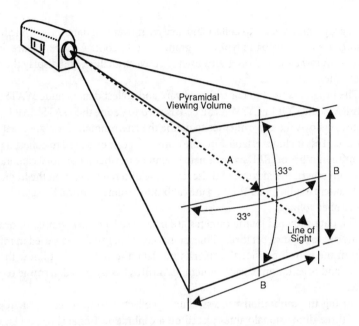

Distance from Camera to Base of Viewing Volume A (in Meters)	Width (and Height) of Base of Viewing Volume B (in Meters)
1.0	0.60
1.4	0.83
2.0	1.2
2.8	1.7
4.0	2.4
5.6	3.3
8.0	4.7

Figure 10. WATSMART Camera Field of View

4x3x250x2 bytes (6K) per second of host computer RAM. A trial lasting 60 seconds would therefore require 6x60 bytes or 360K of available RAM. Since most trials last considerably shorter than 60 seconds and the computer used to collect data contained 640K of RAM, memory requirements did not pose a problem in the present study. The data were processed and analyzed on a Zenith 158 microcomputer equipped with a 20 megabyte hard disk, 640K of RAM, and an Intel 8087 math co-processor.

Software

Several programs are used to collect and analyze movement data with WATSMART. The software is of two basic types: programs used to control the hardware and the collection of raw data; and programs used to convert, analyze, and display the resulting data-files.

The programs used to control hardware and collect data include WATSETUP, CALIBRAT, and COLLECT. WATSETUP is used to define the WATSMART system defaults. It allows the experimenter to define the environment for a given set of experiments. This includes establishing the number of cameras used to collect data; the maximum number of IREDs; the camera orientation (whether or not a camera is upright or inverted); the maximum noise level (the difference between the highest and lowest camera reading for IREDs on the calibration frame); optical linearization; and IRED strober voltage.

The data gathered by the cameras are measured in camera-units. In order for the software to reconstruct three-dimensional coordinate data measured in millimeters from the two-dimensional, camera-unit data, the system must know the exact position and orientation of each camera. CALIBRAT is used to determine these parameters.

During the calibration process, data is collected from a set of 24 IREDs of known three-dimensional values placed on a calibration frame (Figure 11). CALIBRAT uses the readings obtained from each camera to reconstruct three-dimensional coordinates and to determine the error for these reconstructed coordinates. Other diagnostics are also performed, including a display of the dimensional coordinates, gain value, and condition of each calibration frame IRED as seen by each camera; a detailed breakdown of calibration error for each camera and calibration IRED; and a display of the error between the calculated X, Y, and Z coordinates and the actual X, Y, and Z coordinates of all IREDs that can be seen by both cameras.

The COLLECT program allows the experimenter both to prepare the hardware for data collection and to proceed with data collection. The program provides parameters for defining the size of the buffer on the host computer; the length of time to collect data; the data collection frequency in frames per second; filtering frequency; number of IREDs per data frame; number of cameras used in the collection; and various file-naming parameters.

The most important parameters set by the COLLECT program are the collection time, collection frequency, and filtering frequency. The collection time parameter allows the experimenter to determine the length of time during which data will be collected. The collection frequency determines the number of data frames per second.

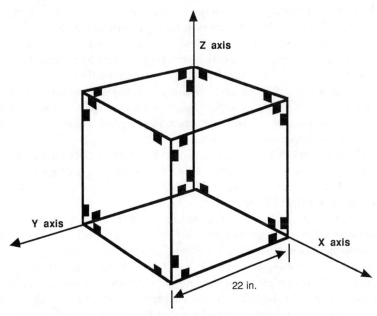

Figure 11. WATSMART Calibration Frame

The data frame is an important concept. A data frame consists of a matrix of values. The size of the matrix is determined by the formula i · j, where i equals the number of IREDs and j the type of data (2- or 3-dimensional). For example, if the data frame contains three IREDs and two-dimensional data, then the data frame would consist of 3 · 2 or 6 values. Each frame represents one "snapshot" of the IREDs; the number of snapshots per second is thus determined by the collection frequency. A collection frequency of 250 Hz would result in a raw data-file containing 250 6-valued frames per second.

The frame is also used to describe reconstructed, three- dimensional data, and the output of any program which manipulates three-dimensional data. These three-dimensional frames are described further in the sample data analysis below.

Several programs are used for data conversion, manipulation, and analysis of movement data collected by WATSMART. CONVERT is used to reconstruct three-dimensional data using direct linear transformation (DLT) techniques. The input to the CONVERT program is two-dimensional data expressed in camera-units; the output is true three-dimensional coordinates. The three-dimensional coordinates are expressed in terms of distance in millimeters from an origin; the origin is 2 to 3 millimeters from the front bottom left corner of the calibration frame. The CON-VERT program assumes that at least two cameras can view each IRED during all of the collected frames; if this is not the case, the experimenter can optionally instruct CONVERT to use a linear spline on all bad sections in the data.

CONVERT and the reconstruction process do not have to be performed on the host computer; any IBM compatible computer can perform the conversion process. The speed at which data reconstruction can take place is determined by the type of computer used and whether a math co-processor is installed. Using the computer equipment described above, the reconstruction procedure utilized in the present study processed approximately 28 IREDs per second.

The output of CONVERT is saved to disk in the form of three-dimensional data frames. Each frame consists of a matrix of values whose size is determined by the number of IREDs. For example, in the present study the three-dimensional data frames are 3 (IREDs) • 3 (axes).

In movement analysis, the experimenter is usually interested in actions with lower maximum frequencies than the collection rate. It is therefore necessary to filter out any higher frequency noise. After reconstruction of three-dimensional data has taken place, the resulting data-files are passed through one of several filtering programs. The filtering programs use a second order Butterworth Filter with a forward and backward pass to filter the data at a frequency determined by the experimenter.

At this point, the data may either be analyzed and displayed or they may require further preparation, depending on the data analysis and display programs to be used. If KINEPLOT is to be used, the three-dimensional filtered data-files must be processed by the TOFLOAT program. This program converts the data-files from integer format to floating point format which allows for greater accuracy.

KINEPLOT is an all-purpose analysis and display program which allows the experimenter to display displacements, velocities, or accelerations on the computer screen or on various hard copy devices. Only minor use was made of KINEPLOT in the present study to obtain initial displays of the data. If KINEPLOT is not used, the prepared data-files are immediately ready for analysis and display. Several programs are available for analyzing the data-files. The most important are SAVEVEL, SAVE-ACC, and DIFFER.

SAVEVEL and SAVEACC calculate the first (velocity) and second (acceleration) derivatives, respectively, of the three-dimensional displacement data. The resulting files are saved to disk in the form of three-dimensional data frames. DIFFER differentiates the X, Y, and Z axes of any input file. If three-dimensional displacement data are the input, the output is three-dimensional instantaneous velocity data; if velocity data are input the resulting output file contains acceleration data. Thus, DIFFER can perform essentially the same function as either SAVEVEL or SAVEACC.

However, it can also be used to differentiate acceleration data-files, thus obtaining
the third derivative (change in acceleration) of displacement, often called "jerk".

DISP and WATSWIND are the most important of the display programs. DISP
plots three-dimensional data-files. The program allows the user to specify the input
file. Options are used to choose which axis to plot, which marker to plot, and scaling.
Scaling can be either automatic or defined by the experimenter. Any combination of
files, axes, or markers may be displayed and each individually scaled or using a uni-
form scale.

An important feature of DISP is the ability to plot resultants for the input data.
For example, if velocity data are the input, the experimenter can use DISP to display
not only velocity in the X, Y, or Z dimension but also the resultant velocity. The program calculates resultants by taking the square root of the sum of squares:

$$R = \sqrt{X^2 + Y^2 + Z^2} \qquad\qquad (EQ1)$$

WATSWIND is used to select a portion of a data-file by determining new start
and end points. This sometimes becomes necessary when extraneous movements at
the beginning or end of a collection trial introduce aberrant values into the data-file.
WATSWIND displays the resultant-velocity profile of a displacement file and allows
the experimenter to save the windowed portion of the file to disk. An overview of
program flow is given in Figure 12.

Sample Data Analysis

This section provides a general description of the process of data analysis. To make
the exposition easier to follow, the analysis of a sample data-file will be described. File
R020.SMS is 30,256 bytes long and contains raw, two-dimensional data. It was collected on May 17, 1987 and represents the eighth trial in which subject SMS produced the fingerspelled word B-U-T five times. The data was collected over a period
of 5.0 seconds at a sampling frequency of 250 Hz.

File R020.SMS is first processed with the CONVERT program to reconstruct
three-dimensional data. This process takes 3.5 minutes and generates file C020.SMS,
which is 22,756 bytes long and contains three-dimensional data frames. A plot of
C020.SMS using DISP is shown in Figure 13. The plot displays the unfiltered, resultant displacement over time of IRED marker 3.

Each data frame for C020.SMS contains a matrix of nine numbers
(3 markers • 3 dimensions). Since the sampling frequency was 250 Hz, there are 250
frames per second. The sampling length was six seconds, so C020.SMS contains

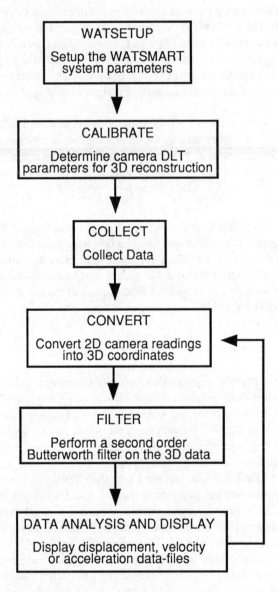

Figure 12. WATSMART Program Flow

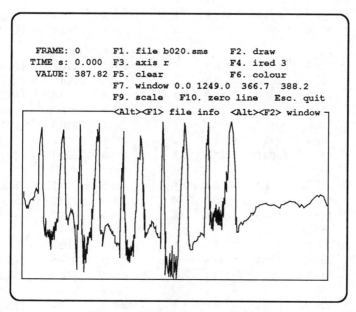

```
FRAME:  0          F1. file b020.sms    F2. draw
TIME s: 0.000      F3. axis r           F4. ired 3
VALUE:  387.82     F5. clear            F6. colour
                   F7. window 0.0 1249.0   366.7  388.2
                   F9. scale   F10. zero line   Esc. quit
         <Alt><F1> file info   <Alt><F2> window
```

Figure 13. Unfiltered Displacement Data

9 • 250 • 6 or 13,500 values. Table 11 lists pertinent information about file C020.SMS and the values for the first 18 frames of displacement data.

Table 11: File C020.SEM̶ Data Dump

Subdirectory: MAY15
Input File: C020.SMS
Output File: 3D020.SMS
Data Type: 1
Date: 5-15-87
Time: 9:55:18
Cameras: 2
Ireds: 3
Frames: 1250
Freq: 250
Filter Cutoff Freq.: 1

WATSCOPE Channels: 0
WATSCOPE Frames: 0
WATSCOPE Freq: 7500
WATSCOPE Gain: 4
Comment: bt-5 reps
Start Frame: 1
Stop Frame: 1250
Start Ired/Chan : 1
Stop Ired/Chan : 3

frame	#1				frame	#10	
1	237.5	213.2	117.0	1	248.9	211.1	114.1

Table 11: File C020.SMS Data Dump (Continued)

2	287.6	222.1	116.5	2	286.3	220.3	115.8
3	213.4	294.5	135.7	3	214.7	289.8	138.9
frame	#2			frame	#11		
1	235.6	212.9	116.9	1	234.0	210.4	114.9
2	286.6	222.3	115.2	2	286.1	220.5	115.5
3	213.8	293.9	136.2	3	214.4	289.4	138.2
frame	#3			frame	#12		
1	236.0	212.7	115.3	1	242.2	210.4	114.2
2	286.4	222.2	115.6	2	285.9	219.9	115.3
3	213.7	293.2	136.9	3	214.0	289.1	138.2
frame	#4			frame	#13		
1	235.0	212.1	116.1	1	239.5	210.2	114.0
2	286.7	221.8	115.6	2	285.9	219.9	114.6
3	214.4	292.5	137.6	3	214.0	288.8	138.3
frame	#5			frame	#14		
1	239.9	212.2	115.5	1	236.1	209.8	114.2
2	286.5	221.7	115.4	2	285.9	219.6	115.3
3	214.0	292.4	137.1	3	213.4	288.3	138.1
frame	#6			frame	#15		
1	236.9	211.2	115.5	1	245.0	210.2	113.5
2	286.3	221.1	115.7	2	285.5	219.6	114.6
3	214.3	291.6	137.7	3	213.8	288.4	138.6
frame	#7			frame	#16		
1	239.6	211.7	114.7	1	239.5	210.1	114.3
2	286.1	221.1	115.4	2	285.5	219.2	114.6
3	214.0	291.3	137.6	3	213.4	288.1	138.6
frame	#8			frame	#17		
1	239.5	211.3	114.8	1	243.2	209.9	114.5
2	286.5	220.9	115.5	2	285.5	219.2	114.6
3	214.9	290.9	138.5	3	213.2	287.7	137.9
frame	#9			frame	#18		
1	243.1	211.0	115.0	1	242.4	209.6	113.7
2	286.1	220.7	114.8	2	285.3	219.2	114.4
3	214.5	290.3	138.6	3	213.0	287.5	138.3

C020.SMS is filtered at a frequency of 1 Hz using BFILTER. The process takes approximately 30 seconds and yields a filtered data-file, B020.SMS, which is 45,280 bytes long. File B020.SMS can now be used to obtain accurate displacement data. Figure 14 displays filtered displacement data.

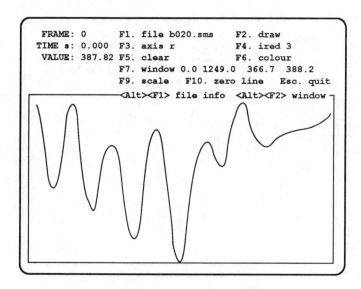

Figure 14. Filtered Displacement Data

File B020.SMS can now be analyzed further by processing it with SAVEVEL and SAVEACC. Each program takes approximately 15 seconds to perform the analysis and writes two more data-files, V020.SMS and A020.SMS, each 45,280 bytes long. These files can be displayed using DISP to obtain information about velocity, acceleration, and timings. Figure 15 displays the resultant velocity of IRED marker 3 over time.

DISP can also be used to display complex relationships among data-files, axes, and markers. Figure 16 shows both the displacements (B020.SMS) and the velocities (V020.SMS) for marker 3, the index finger. Again, resultant displacements and velocities have been plotted rather than displacement or velocity in any one axis. The plots have been superimposed so that the relative timings can be seen. Thus, it is possible to note when the peak velocities occur relative to displacement. Figure 8 is an edited version of Figure 7 and identifies these points. Both velocity and displacement have been scaled independently so that all data points from both files will appear on the plot. Because of this, it is not possible to compare velocity and displacement values. In Figure 8, horizontal tick marks indicate the points of peak velocities and vertical tick marks indicate velocity minima.

DISP can also be used to obtain precise values for all displayed data. For example, Figure 17 revealed that peak velocity occurs approximately one-half to three-

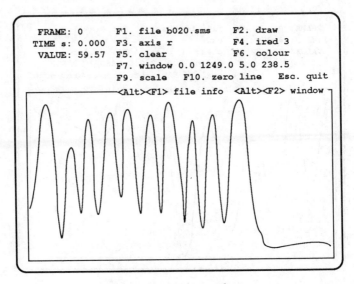

```
FRAME:  0        F1. file b020.sms    F2. draw
TIME s: 0.000    F3. axis r           F4. ired 3
VALUE:  59.57    F5. clear            F6. colour
                 F7. window 0.0 1249.0 5.0 238.5
                 F9. scale   F10. zero line   Esc. quit
               <Alt><F1> file info  <Alt><F2> window
```

Figure 15. Velocity Plot

quarters of the way through the movement. To find out the precise timing of the peak velocity the following procedure can be used.

Using DISP, the experimenter positions the computer's cursor on the displacement plot. The arrow keys can then be used to move through the data frames, one frame at a time. Frame number, time in seconds, and displayed value can be observed in the upper left corner of the DISP display. Moving the cursor to the first displacement valley reveals that it occurs at time 0.476. The following displacement peak occurs at time 0.772. Thus, the total time taken by the subject to move the index finger was 0.296 seconds. Switching to the velocity plot, the same procedure reveals that the velocity peak for this movement occurred at time 0.660, or 0.184 seconds into the movement. Thus, it is possible to calculate that the velocity peak occurred 62% of the way through the displacement movement.

With these procedures, the number of values to be computed and analyzed accumulates quickly. In the present study, a total of 175 seconds of data were collected. Each second of three-dimensional data consists of 250 frames with nine values, or 2,250 values per second. Thus, a total of 393,750 displacement values were collected. Since each displacement file often is processed to obtain a velocity and an acceleration data-file, and since each of these three files can also be used to calculate resultants, the present study contains well over one million data points.

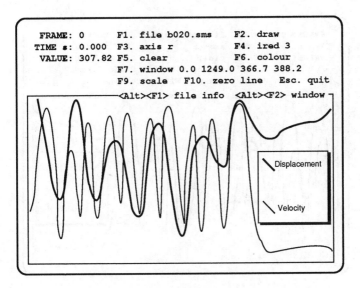

```
FRAME: 0          F1. file b020.sms     F2. draw
TIME s: 0.000     F3. axis r            F4. ired 3
VALUE: 307.82     F5. clear             F6. colour
                  F7. window 0.0 1249.0 366.7 388.2
                  F9. scale   F10. zero line   Esc. quit
         <Alt><F1> file info   <Alt><F2> window
```

Displacement

Velocity

Figure 16. Displacement and Velocity Plot

Methods and Procedures for Motion Analysis Studies

Subjects

Three adults served as subjects for the collection of fingerspelling and loan sign data. All three were deaf and had deaf spouses. Two of the subjects were female; one was male. All three were right hand dominant signers.

Stimulus Materials

Data was collected for eight simple fingerspelled and loan sign words. Table 12 summarizes the data collection for these studies.

Column one lists the word that is being produced; column two lists the subject; column three gives the data collection time; column four lists the repetitions or other variables associated with that set of trials; and the last column lists the number of trials. In the Rep/Variables column, a number represents the number of times a partic-

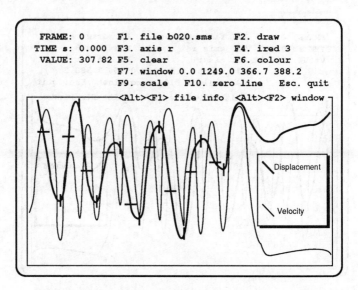

Figure 17. Displacement and Velocity Plot (edited version)

Table 12: Data Overview

Word	Subject	Time	Rep/ Variables	Trials
#TB	SMS	2.5	1	7
#TB	TLS	2.5	1	5
#TB	BAH	2.5	1	6
#TB	SMS	6.0	5	5
#TB	TLS	5.0	5	5
#TB	BAH	5.0	5	5
BUT	SMS	2.5	1	5
BUT	TLS	2.5	1	5
BUT	BAH	2.5	1	5
BUT	SMS	5.0	5	5
BUT	TLS	5.0	5	5
BUT	BAH	4.0	5	5
BO	SMS	10.0	RC[a]	2
OB	SMS	10.0	RC	2

Table 12: Data Overview (Continued)

Word	Subject	Time	Rep/ Variables	Trials
BO	TLS	10.0	RC	2
OB	TLS	10.0	RC	2
BO	BAH	10.0	RC	2
OB	BAH	10.0	RC	3
SHE	SMS	2.5	SLOW	2
SHE	SMS	2.5	NORM	2
SHE	SMS	2.5	FAST	4
SHE	TLS	2.5	SLOW	2
SHE	TLS	2.5	NORM	2
SHE	TLS	2.5	FAST	3
SHE	BAH	2.5	SLOW	3
SHE	BAH	2.5	NORM	2
SHE	BAH	2.5	FAST	2
SUE	SMS	2.5	SLOW	3
SUE	SMS	2.5	NORM	3
SUE	SMS	2.5	FAST	3
SUE	BAH	2.5	SLOW	2
SUE	BAH	2.5	NORM	2
SUE	BAH	2.5	FAST	3
COCONUT	BAH	6.0	—	2
COCONUT	SMS	6.0	3	3
BANANA	BAH	6.0	—	3
BANANA	SMS	6.0	3	2

a. RC stands for Rate Change

ular word was repeated. For example, in the fourth row, the loan sign #TOO-BAD (TB) was repeated five times. In some instances, words were fingerspelled at three rates: slow, normal, and fast. In other instances, the subjects were instructed to start fingerspelling a sequence of letters slowly and to speed up gradually over a specified length of time.

Marker Placement and Attachment

Three IRED-markers were used in this study. Marker 1 was attached to the subject's thumb; marker 2 was attached to the fleshy portion of the hand between the thumb and the index finger; and marker 3 was attached to the middle section of the subject's index finger. Figure 10 shows the location of the markers.

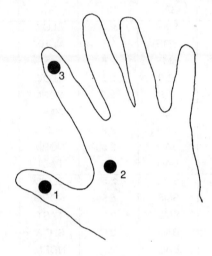

Figure 10. Marker Placement

Markers were attached to the subjects with a tacky, putty-like material commonly used for temporarily hanging pictures or posters on walls. A "ring" was formed from the material and wrapped around the subject's index finger and thumb. A small portion of the material was then also pressed firmly onto the marker, and this was in turn pressed onto the ring. Marker two was attached only by pressing a small amount of the material onto the marker and then pressing the marker against the skin. The connecting wires were held in place with tape at the subject's wrist and routed from there to the strober controller, which was allowed to rest on the table.

Sampling Times and Rates

As described in Table 12, data sampling times varied from a minimum of 2.5 seconds to a maximum of 10 seconds. All data were collected at a sampling frequency rate of 250 Hz.

Room and Camera Arrangement

All movement data were collected in the Kinesiology Laboratory at the University of Colorado at Boulder. It was not possible to adjust the room and camera arrangements. Because of the fixed camera positions, strict restraints were placed on what words could be used as data and on the arm and hand positions of the subjects. In order to collect data, the cameras must be able to view the IREDs during most of the articulatory movement. If for any reason a marker is obscured from the view of a camera, loss of data results. The splining procedure available in CONVERT can compensate for some loss of data, but the experimenter must ensure that gaps resulting from obscured markers are of as short a duration as possible. In an optimal experimental situation, the cameras would be repositioned for each trial, although this would also mean that the calibration procedure would have to be performed for each trial.

In the present study, the cameras were positioned overhead approximately two meters from the subject. Subjects were allowed to sit, resting their right arm on a table; from this position, they could watch the experimenter signal when to start fingerspelling. This did not provide an ideal arm position for completely natural fingerspelling; however, since the words which the subjects were asked to fingerspell were very simple, it is doubtful that these constraints affected the actual fingerspelling movements in any significant way. It was the impression of the experimenter and the other subjects, who were present throughout the entire study, that the fingerspelling was natural and comprehensible.

Calibration

The entire set of data was collected over a two-day period. Each time the WATSMART equipment is turned on or moved, the calibration procedure must be performed, and so two calibrations were necessary for the present study.

The WATSMART technical manual recommends that when the cameras are at a distance of one meter from the calibration frame the calibration error should be less than 3.0 millimeters. As the distance increases the calibration error also increases. In the present configuration, the cameras were approximately two meters from the calibration frame. The associated calibration errors of 4.69 millimeters for the first day of data collection and 3.97 millimeters for the second day were within acceptable limits.

Chapter 4
Targets and Transitions

Models Revisited

We have seen that a cipher model of fingerspelling which characterizes the structure of fingerspelled words as merely a sequence of static handshapes corresponding to English printed letters is inadequate to explain how fingerspelling is produced, perceived, and comprehended. Fingerspelling must be described phonetically in terms of its constitutive gestures, their sequential transmission, and their influence on each other.

Akamatsu's (1982, 1985) movement envelope model, while an advance over the cipher model, is still primarily formulated in terms of static hand configurations and their serial concatenation. It leaves unanswered the essential question of how the movements of movement envelopes are organized. The critical question for a movement envelope model of fingerspelling is how to incorporate movement. The question was put in the first chapter: How are letters put into movement envelopes? Assume for the moment that a fingerspelled word consists of a series of canonical handshape targets with transitional movements between the targets. The fingerspelled word BANK consists of four targets, corresponding to the fingerspelled letters B, A, N, and K, and the transitions between them (the transition between B and A, A and N, and so forth).

Like Akamatsu's movement envelope model, this model of fingerspelling recognizes that fingerspelling is more than a series of discrete, static handshapes. The hand configurations of fingerspelled letters function as articulatory targets. They serve as goals, or modulation points, along a moving trajectory. The articulatory motions of fingerspelling, according to this view, are movements into and out of these targets.

This preliminary model of fingerspelling in terms of targets and transitions is admittedly too simple. Several problems must be considered if it is to be developed into an adequate model. First is the problem of characterizing the targets. Two alternatives may be proposed: characterizing targets in terms of spatial locations or in terms of hand configurations.

The spatial location alternative is not unreasonable. Spatial locations for movement can be accurately perceived and attained (Kelso, Holt, and Flatt, 1980; Wallace, 1977). In addition, spatial locations are known to be important in both the lexicon and the grammar ASL (Stokoe, 1960; Klima and Bellugi, 1979; Poizner, Newkirk, and Bellugi, 1983).

Spatial locations as articulatory targets have also been posited in the organization of speech articulation (MacNeilage, 1970), but they do not seem as significant as configurations of articulators. A convincing demonstration of this is the fact that we can understand speech produced under extraordinary conditions, such as when someone talks while holding a pipe between his teeth. Obviously, the spatial locations are quite different than would be produced under normal circumstances, yet we have no problem understanding the speech. Bite-block experiments have confirmed that although articulators may not attain their canonical locations, the overall goal of the system — comprehensible speech sounds — can still be achieved (Fowler and Turvey, 1980; Kelso and Tuller, 1983; Lindblom and Sundberg, 1971).

In the case of fingerspelling, the coding of spatial locations may turn out to be more similar to speech than it is ASL. Defining fingerspelling targets in terms of their spatial locations would be exceedingly complex; in addition, it would imply that productions made at different spatial locations (the letter A produced close versus farther from the body) would be different letters, which they clearly are not.

Related to this is the question of what makes a target. Targets are not only handshapes; orientations and, as we will see below, even movements are important features of targets. Even in the case of handshapes, quite detailed phonetic features of individual articulators must be specified. Finally, we cannot overlook the relations, both spatial and temporal, among articulators. Configurations of articulators, and the relations among configurations, are clearly more important in the characterization of fingerspelling targets than actual, three-dimensional spatial locations.

A second problem in characterizing targets is the identification of a canonical form. It is unlikely that invariant handshapes can be identified. The articulatory gestures of fingerspelling are subject to the same coarticulatory effects that we find in speech, where the search for invariants has also been a problem. Various models of coarticulation attempt to deal with the problem of invariance in different ways. In the articulatory model of speech proposed by Henke (1966), input is assumed to be a string of segments characterized as a specific set of articulatory goals. The targets are invariant, environment-independent shapes and positions of articulators. Although the articulators move toward these targets, the precise form may not be attained. Factors which affect the precise targets which are reached include the past positions and shapes of the articulators and the timing of the sequential inputs.

Fowler (1980, 1984) proposes a different approach to understanding how speech is segmented in spite of coarticulation. According to Fowler, listeners "segment the speech stream along its coarticulatory lines into overlapping phonetic segments" (1984:361). Segments are perceived, not at the point where a segment's salience predominates the signal, but at the point where the one segment ceases to dominate the signal and another takes over.[1] Coarticulation thus does not smear the discrete character of segments, but preserves the coherence of the temporally extended parts of individual phonetic segments.

The phenomenon of coarticulation provides strong counter-evidence to a conception of speech or fingerspelling targets as static structures. As Anderson (1974:5) notes:

> In fact, the vocal organs are all continually in motion, and at any given point in time, they are likely to be executing gestures associated not with one but with several of the segments of an utterance. That is, the organs do not simply adopt a static position, hold it briefly, and then move to another position, but rather, during the period associated with one segment, they are already moving into position for a segment to follow.

The same phenomenon is true for fingerspelling. If we observe actual fingerspelling, it appears that there is no period during which the hand forms a static handshape. A simple examination of a displacement plot bears this out. In Figure 18, for example, the smooth displacement curve indicates that the index finger is in constant motion. Lack of motion (and thus evidence for a substantial period during which the hand was forming a static handshape) would appear on the plot as a long, horizontal portion of the curve. No evidence for long periods of stasis exist in any of the data collected.

The characterization of transitions seems easier. We might assume at first that transitions are merely the movements to and from targets. Unlike targets, transitions are not the critical components of fingerspelling. The targets are what correspond to English letters. They are, in this sense, the significant information. Transitions are predictable from linguistic or physiological constraints, and thus are less informative than targets.

Similar arguments have been presented concerning transitions versus targets in speech. Anderson (1974:5) summarizes these arguments by noting that speech can be represented in such a way that:

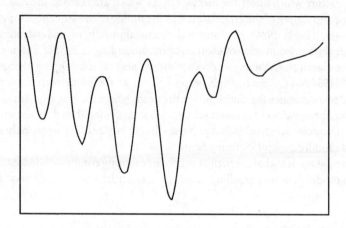

Figure 18. Displacement Plot, Marker Three.

> the utterance is a sequence of a finite number of discrete, homoge-
> neously characterizable, atomic segments, rather than as a continuum. For
> instance, each segment is characterized in terms of a state of the vocal or-
> gans, and the transitions between these states are assumed to be predictable
> in terms of very general linguistic and physiological laws.

Problems arise, however, for such a characterization of transitions. In first- and
second-language acquisition and in fluent perception of fingerspelling, it is not the
individual letters that need to be attended to but the "whole word" or movement envelope. For deaf children learning to fingerspell, as we saw in the first chapter, the
movement envelope constitutes an important production and perceptual unit even
before they have knowledge of the correspondence between fingerspelling handshapes and English letters.

An analogous situation arises in the acquisition of speech. Children often acquire units which are not equivalent to, and most often larger than, the units manipulated by adults. It is only later in the child's development that these wholistic units
are segmented (Peters, 1983:89).

Second, fingerspelling is a rhythmic activity. Factors such as tempo and evenness are as important in fingerspelling as they are in speech and serve as evidence that
movement is often directly manipulated in fingerspelling. Jerky versus smooth fingerspelling is easily detected and often is used to characterize fingerspelling as fluent
or non-fluent. This suggests that parameters associated with movement between tar-

gets may serve as points of control, a prediction also noted by Turvey (1980:53): "speaking and signing, like movement in general, are necessarily rhythmical suggesting, perhaps, that their formational aspects are nontrivially determined by strictures of cyclicity such as mutual synchronization." The issue of synchronization and dynamic control will be considered in detail in the following chapter. For now, it is sufficient to note that movement between targets may be a factor that is critically and directly controlled. A view of fingerspelling which considers transitions as entirely predictable movements to and from targets will not be adequate.

What this implies is that, in some instances, transitions may function as "targets." We know that this is the case for two fingerspelled letters, J and Z, where movement is the criterial feature. It may also be true that certain distinctive fingerspelling movements become target units to be produced. An example of movements which may function as targets can be found in the two characteristic gestures of J-O-H-N (the orientational changes associated with the J-to-O and the H-to-N gestures). In loan signs, examples abound: the characteristic movements of #EARLY, #CONN (abbreviation for Connecticut), #BACK, #TOO-BAD, and so forth.

The Salience of Targets and Transitions

The model described above poses interesting questions concerning the relative informational load of targets versus transitions. Consider the relative timings of targets and transitions. If the targets of fingerspelled words are only briefly achieved, then much of the time spent in fingerspelling is in transitional movements. If we ask which unit is likely to be more salient, the targets or the transitions, a reasonable answer would be that the temporally longer transitions may carry a substantial portion of the information in a fingerspelled word. Further, if transitions in fingerspelling are salient and informative, this could explain why it is so often noted that proficient fingerspelling comprehension depends on seeing more than just individual letters. Perhaps the additional information so necessary to perception of fingerspelling is contained within the transitions between letters.

In fact, there are sound theoretical reasons to predict that transitions in fingerspelling and in speech are informative and not mere noise. This issue will be discussed in the next section. For now, it will be worthwhile merely to determine whether transitions are temporally longer than targets.

A representative corpus of data for simple fingerspelling and loan sign movements was selected. This corpus consisted of data-files containing the words B-U-T and #TOO-BAD, produced five times each by subjects SMS and TLS.[2] An overview of the corpus of data appears in Table 13.

Table 13: Target/Transition Data Overview

Subject	Word	# of Files
SMS	TOO-BAD	5
SMS	BUT	5
TLS	TOO-BAD	4
TLS	BUT	5

For these simple words, movement of marker 3 (the index finger) can be used to locate target positions. In the fluent production of these items, no point could be located during which the articulators were not in motion; that is, there is no point in the data where the displacement remain stable over time. Therefore, the following method was used to measure the timings of targets and transitions.

The method is illustrated in Figure 19. First, displacement peaks were located,

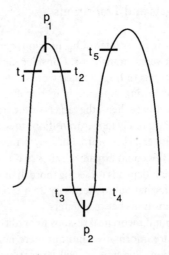

Figure 19. Target and Transition Measurement

corresponding to maximally open and closed hand positions, B and T respectively (points p_1 and p_2). Next, displacements of 1 millimeter in each direction (approaching and leaving) relative to this peak were located and their times noted (times t_1, t_2,

t_3, and t_4).[3] These times were then used to calculate the timings for both targets and transitions. To calculate the timing for the first target, the formula was:

$$T_{target} = t_2 - t_1 \tag{EQ2}$$

The timing for the first transition was calculated with the formula:

$$T_{trans} = t_3 - t_2. \tag{EQ3}$$

Timings for targets and transitions across words and segments (targets and transitions) are given in Table 14. A two-way (Segment X Word) analysis of variance

Table 14: Target and Transition Timings

Variable	Label	Mean	Std Dev	Cases
Segment	Targets	.0912	.0512	156
Word	TOO-BAD	.0784	.0431	77
Word	BUT	.1038	.0556	79
Segment	Transitions	.3140	.1160	136
Word	TOO-BAD	.3091	.1111	67
Word	BUT	.3188	.1211	69

was performed on the data. The results are shown in Table 15.

Transitions lasted an average of 314 milliseconds; targets lasted for an average of 91 milliseconds. This difference was significant, $F_{(1,291)} = 473.294$, $p < .001$.

These results do not prove that transitions are more perceptually salient than targets. Indeed, the results must interpreted with caution, since the identification of targets and transitions was ad hoc. The results do suggest, however, that transitions comprise a significant portion of the phonetic structure of fingerspelling and will have to be considered in models of its articulatory organization.

These results also are meaningful for second language learners. If learners are looking for static, canonical, and invariant hand configurations, then it is little wonder why understanding fingerspelling is so difficult. They are looking for something that simply is not there.

Table 15: Analysis of Variance Results

Source of Variation	Sum of Squares	DF	Mean Square	F	Signif. of F
Main Effects	3.631	2	1.816	238.249	.000
SEG	3.607	1	3.607	473.294	.000
WORD	.024	1	.024	3.132	.078
2-way Interactions	.004	1	.004	.590	.443
SEG WORD	.004	1	.004	.590	.443
Explained	3.635	3	1.212	159.030	.000
Residual	2.195	288	.008		
Total	5.830	291	.020		

Dynamic Modeling of Phonetic Structure

The model of fingerspelling being developed here suggests that transitions are critical, informative components of the overall signal. The notion that transitions are salient, informative units of the speech signal has also been proposed. Fowler (1984) hinted at this in her suggestion that it is not the points of maximum prominence that are perceptually salient, but the points where a segment can first be detected. While maximum prominence may be a feature of targets, initial detection of a segment could occur during transitions.

One suggestion that transitions are important appears in Dew and Jensen (1977:115-116):

> The speech production mechanism is a target-oriented system.... The act of production is regarded as a process of adjusting from one target to the next, and the adjustment between targets is referred to as a transition.... The transitions between targets are not merely simple by-products of the articulatory act but often constitute significant cues in themselves about their intended targets by virtue of their trajectories.

The notion that speech must be understood in terms of the coordinated production of articulatory trajectories can be extended even farther. A framework based on dynamic modeling of speech is beginning to emerge which has direct implications for models of fingerspelling. Browman and Goldstein (1985:35) present the basic tenets of the framework:

> Much linguistic phonetic research has attempted to characterize phonetic units in terms of measurable physical parameters or features. Basic to these approaches is the view that a phonetic description consists of a linear sequence of static physical measures, either articulatory configurations or acoustical parameters. The course of movement from one such configuration to another has been viewed as secondary. We have proposed an alternative approach, one that characterizes phonetic structure as patterns of articulatory movement, or gestures, rather than static configurations. While the traditional approaches have viewed the continuous movement of vocal-tract articulators over time as "noise" that tends to obscure the segment-like structure of speech, we have argued that setting out to characterize articulator movement directly leads not to noise but to organized spatiotemporal structures that can be used as the basis for phonological generalizations as well as accurate physical description. In our view, then, a phonetic representation is a characterization of how a physical system (e.g., a vocal tract) changes over time.

A fundamental concept of the dynamic view is that speech is the coordinated activity of a multi-degree of freedom system (Kelso, 1986). At issue is how this complex system is controlled. According to the dynamic view, functional groupings of muscles and joints form coordinative structures, ensembles of articulators that work cooperatively as a single, task-specific unit (Kelso, Tuller, Vatikiotis-Bateson, and Fowler, 1984). According to proponents of the dynamic view, coordinated movements are not controlled in an algorithmic, servo-mechanical way, where a master "program" compares a system's state against some master plan, perhaps stated in terms of spatial targets, and adjusts it accordingly. Rather, these systems "consist of ensembles of coupled and mutually entrained oscillators and ... coordination is a natural consequence of this organization" (Kelso, Tuller, and Harris, 1983:140).

The dynamic view of speech production has several implications for a model of fingerspelling. First, the view characterizes speech at a level of organization, that of articulatory trajectories, which can be applied quite generally. Coordinative structures have been located not only in speech, but across speech and manual activities (Kelso, Tuller, and Harris, 1983); in non-linguistic (finger-tapping) and linguistic (writing) manual activities (Haken, Kelso, and Bunz, 1985; Viviani and Terzuolo, 1980); and even in animal behavior (Fukson, Berkinblit, and Fel'dman, 1980; Pearson, 1976). The search for coordinative structures indicative of a dynamic organization of fingerspelling is entirely appropriate. In fact, such an organization is actually predicted by the dynamic view, which suggests that "there may be nothing special, a priori, about neural structures and their 'wiring' that mandates the existence of co-ordinative structures. Rather, it suggests that the functional cooperativity, not the neural mechanism per se, is fundamental" (Kelso, Saltzman, and Tuller, 1986:33). That is, the dynamic system itself is the underlying structure; language, whether at the level of neural processes or overt, phonetic representations, merely instantiates this underlying system.

In summary, the dynamic model seeks to explain speech production in terms of control and cooperativity. Control of individual articulators takes place by limiting the degrees of freedom of a complex system. Cooperativity results from the entrain-ment of articulators characteristic of coordinative structures. Control and coordina-tion are factors which are critical in fluent fingerspelling. They will be explored, with a view towards determining whether support can be found for a dynamic model of fingerspelling, in the following chapter.

Chapter 5
Towards a Dynamics
of Fingerspelling

From Kinematics to Dynamics

Dynamics, as it is applied within the field of speech production and human movement in general, seeks to describe how complex systems are controlled. One source
of evidence for dynamic control is the fact that systems with many degrees of freedom act in a cooperative, coordinated fashion.

Data will be presented in this chapter which provide preliminary support for a
dynamic theory of fingerspelling production. One way to demonstrate that fingerspelling is controlled dynamically is to look for evidence of cooperativity among the
articulators used to produce fingerspelled words. Two lines of evidence will be presented which suggest that such cooperativity exists. First, however, we will examine
several kinematic features of fingerspelling.

Fingerspelling Speed

In the context of fingerspelling, three types of speed are relevant. First, speed of fingerspelling can be measured by dividing the distance travelled by the elapsed time.
This will be called the *average speed* of fingerspelling. Another measure of speed of
fingerspelling is the mean of the maximum instantaneous velocity of the articulators.
This measurement will be called the *mean peak velocity*. Finally, the speed fingerspelling may be measured by calculating the number of letters produced in a certain
amount of time. This type of speed will be referred to as the *rate* of fingerspelling.

Prior estimates of the speed of fingerspelling have relied solely on the rate of fingerspelling method. Rates reported in the literature have averaged from approxi-

mately 160 to 200 milliseconds per letter. Measuring the rate of fingerspelling in the present data will provide a check of previously reported estimates using more precisely measured data and, if the rates are found to be similar, confirmation that these data are representative of natural fingerspelling.

The present data was analyzed for all three kinematic parameters. Four data-files of the fingerspelled word B-U-T were used as the corpus of data for measuring average speed. The corpus included two data-files from subject SMS and two from subject TLS. Average speed was calculated by dividing the resultant distance that marker 3 travelled by the elapsed time.

The measurement of average speed is sensitive both to the sizes of the articulators and the placement of the markers. Thus, smaller articulators or placement of markers closer to the hand (larger articulators or placement of markers closer to the fingertips) will result in smaller (larger) average speeds. Both of these factors varied considerably for these data. Subject SMS, a female, had smaller hands than TLS, a male. Also, precise placement of the markers — for example in terms of relative distance from the fingertips — was not taken into consideration. Results are reported by subject.

Finally, peak velocity was measured directly from the velocity plots generated by DISP for subjects' SMS and TLS production of the fingerspelled word B-U-T. Seven data-files were used with a total of 56 velocity peaks. The individual peak velocities were grouped according to subject.

Results for average speed are given in Table 16. For subject SMS, the average speed was 28.485 mm/sec. As expected because of hand size and marker placement, subject TLS's average speed was faster, 47.763 mm/sec..

Table 16: Average Speed

Subject	Mean	St. Dev.	Max	Min
SMS	28.485	11.204	48.028	10.897
TLS	47.763	15.571	75.392	26.302

Overall results for the mean peak velocity measurement are given in Table 17. The mean peak velocity for both subjects was 242 mm/sec.

Peak velocities were compared across subjects to determine whether the subjects' peak velocities differed significantly. Results of the t-test are given in Table 18.

Subject SMS had a mean peak velocity of 219 mm/sec. Subject TLS's mean peak velocity was significantly faster ($t = 4.32$, $p < .001$) at 274 mm/sec.

Table 17: Average Peak Velocity

Mean	St.Dev.	Max	Min
242.23	60.02	514.59	129.77

Table 18: t-Test Results, Overall Peak Velocity

Subject	Number of Cases	Mean	Standard Deviation	Standard Error
SMS	38	219.3268	60.664	9.841
TLS	27	274.4570	42.249	8.131

t value	Degrees of Freedom	2-Tail Probability
−4.32	63	.000

The results of the analysis of fingerspelling speed must be interpreted with caution. Since the measurement is sensitive to hand size and marker placement, it is difficult to compare the speeds reported across subjects. In addition, speed within subjects varies considerably. The range for subject SMS was from approximately 10 to 48 mm/sec; for subject TLS, the range was approximately 26 to 75 mm/sec.

The results indicating that the mean peak velocities of the subjects were significantly different need to be explored further. Is this finding consistent across productions, or the result of one atypically fast or slow production? The means of each production are given in Table 19.

A one-way analysis of variance was performed to compare the means of the seven sets of peak velocity data-files, and a post hoc Scheffe's test was applied to determine the source of the difference.

The results indicate that of the seven productions, the only significant difference occurred between one production of subject TLS (number 2, see Table 19) and three productions of subject SMS (numbers 1, 3, and 4, see Table 19). Thus, the peak velocities of the subjects were much more similar than the figures in Table 18 would lead us to believe.

The measurement of fingerspelling rate was made by dividing the number of letters produced by the total time taken. Three data-files were used (trials 19 and 20 of TLS, and trial 22 of SMS). To find the total time, the time of the first maximum

Table 19: Main Peak Velocity by Production

Subject	Count	Mean	Standard Deviation	Standard Error
SMS(1)	9	182.0022	22.1752	7.3917
SMS(2)	10	257.6880	92.2738	29.1795
SMS(3)	10	228.1690	29.7181	9.3977
SMS(4)	9	204.2033	46.8454	15.6151
TLS(1)	9	242.7278	14.6458	4.8819
TLS(2)	9	318.1644	41.0206	13.6735
TLS(3)	9	262.4789	21.4676	7.1559
Total	65	242.2271	60.0191	7.4445

velocity peak for marker 3 was subtracted from the time of the final maximum velocity peak for the same marker.[1] Results are given in Table 20.

Table 20: Fingerspelling Rates

Trial	Rate	Time
SMS22	5.102	2.940
TLS19	4.524	3.316
TLS20	4.438	3.380
Std Dev	0.36	0.238
Mean	4.69	3.212

The mean rate of 4.69 letters per second is equivalent to a mean fingerspelling rate of 213 milliseconds per letter. This rate accords well with the average rate of 160–200 milliseconds per letter reported in the literature.

Cooperativity in Fingerspelling Production

In the change in perspective from a kinematic description to a dynamic explanation of fingerspelling, we cease to look at the surface characteristics of the motions and begin instead to search for more abstract sources of control in the complex system of movements at work in fingerspelling. One place we could begin to search for controlled parameters is speed, especially fingerspelling rate and peak velocity.

One method for exploring the issue of control is to compare and contrast data from productions of fluent and non-fluent fingerspelling. Areas of control should appear in fluent fingerspelling but not in non-fluent fingerspelling. As we have seen, a common belief, especially among beginners, is that fluent fingerspelling is somehow faster than non-fluent fingerspelling. We could predict, therefore, that fluent fingerspelling will be characterized by faster fingerspelling rates and average peak velocities than non-fluent fingerspelling.

As fingerspelling data was being collected for these studies, the experimenter made entries in a log concerning any special conditions pertaining to each trial. Some of these entries commented on the subject's fingerspelling fluency. In particular, it was noted that in four trials the subjects produced noticeably non-fluent fingerspelling. Often, these productions were the first trials in a new task. The non-fluencies were not severe disruptions and did not result in "slips of the hand" (Fromkin, 1980); that is, the resulting productions did not incorporate anticipation, perseveration, or metathesis of segments. They did, however, result in a noticeable lack of control.[2] These non-fluent productions consisted of trial 13 of subject SMS (fingerspelled B-U-T, one repetition); trial 18 of subject SMS (fingerspelled B-U-T, five repetitions); and, trials 16 and 17 of subject TLS (fingerspelled B-U-T, four repetitions for trial 16 and five repetitions for trial 17).

To test whether fingerspelling rate is a controlled variable, the rates of the fluent and non-fluent productions were compared. The method used to calculate the fingerspelling rates was explained above. The same fluent productions were used. For the non-fluent productions, three data-files were used (trials 16 and 17 of TLS, and trial 18 of SMS). Results are given in Table 21.

There is very little difference between fingerspelling rates of fluent and non-fluent fingerspelling ($t = 0.98$, $p = 0.384$). In fluent word production, 4.69 letters were produced each second, resulting in an average sending rate of 213 milliseconds per letter. For the non-fluent words, 4.41 letters were produced each second, or 227 milliseconds per letter.[3] Rate of fingerspelling does not appear to be one of the parameters under control in fluent versus non-fluent fingerspelling.

Table 21: Fluent versus Non-Fluent Fingerspelling Rates

| Fluent | | Non-Fluent | | Trial[a] |
Rate	Time	Rate	Time	
5.102	2.940	4.433	3.384	SMS18
4.524	3.316	4.732	2.536	TLS16
4.438	3.380	4.067	3.688	TLS17
0.36	0.238	0.33	0.597	**Std Dev**
4.69	3.212	4.41	3.203	**Mean**

a. Trial numbers are for non-fluent data only; fluent trial numbers are the same as
those listed in Table 20.

In order to examine peak velocity, data from non-fluent fingerspelling (trials 13
and 18 of SMS, and trials 16 and 17 of TLS) was compared to a set of fluent productions which was selected from neighboring trials (trials 18 and 22 of SMS, and trials
19 and 20 of TLS). The values are given in Table 22.

Table 22: t-Test Results, Peak Velocities

Category	Mean	Standard Deviation	Standard Error
Fluent	245.7689	62.506	11.813
Non-fluent	343.0659	67.139	12.921
t Value	Degrees of Freedom	2-Tail Probability	
-5.56	53	.000	

The results show that fluent fingerspelling has significantly slower peak velocities (246 mm/sec) than non-fluent (343 mm/sec), t = 5.56, p < .001.

These results seem counterintuitive, until we realize that the faster peak velocities of non-fluent fingerspelling may be the result of a lack of control. That is, they
may indicate uneven, jerky movements. If this is true, then the important factor for

determining whether peak velocity is controlled in fingerspelling is not the absolute value of the mean peak velocities but the degree of variability among peak velocities. Low variability in fluent fingerspelling, and high variability in non-fluent fingerspelling, would be evidence that peak velocity is a controlled factor.

The following method was used to measure the degree of variability in peak velocities. First, peak velocities for each marker were measured on the velocity plots of each data-file; the mean peak velocity for each marker was calculated. Next, variability of peak velocities was derived by taking the absolute value of the difference of individual peak velocities and the mean; this calculation was repeated for each marker across all the data-files. The formula used to calculate peak velocity variability is:

$$PV_{var} = \left| PV_i - \overline{PV} \right| \qquad \text{(EQ4)}$$

The resulting values were used as the measure of variability. Mean values for fluent and non-fluent fingerspelling are given in Table 23 (mean values given in mm/seconds).

Table 23: Peak Velocity Variability, Fluent versus Non-Fluent

Category	Mean	Standard Deviation	Standard Error
Fluent	36.9655	43.979	3.640
Non-fluent	14.1147	14.503	1.176

t Value	Degrees of Freedom	2-Tail Probability
5.97	175	.000

The results of a t-test indicate that fluent productions were characterized by significantly less variability in peak velocities, t = 5.97, p < .001.

The data presented above can be understood in terms of rhythmic control. Cooperativity among articulators results in an overall evenness to fingerspelling motions. The peak velocities of an individual articulator over time tends to show little variability. In non-fluent fingerspelling, where such cooperativity is lacking, the variability of peak velocities is much greater, resulting in an uneven, jerky production.

Control of peak velocities is one indication that cooperativity among articulators is present in fingerspelling. Further evidence of control, and one which is an even a stronger indication of an underlying dynamic organization to fingerspelling, is the temporal synchronicity of individual articulators. The phenomenon is best illustrated by examining velocity plots of fluent and non-fluent fingerspelling.

Figure 20 shows a plot of trial 14 (SMS), an example of fluent fingerspelling. The important feature to notice is the timings of the articulators at their peak velocities. Although the peak velocities of each articulator do not coincide precisely, a high degree of temporal co-occurrence can be observed. When the subject's index finger is moving its fastest, so are the thumb and the hand (although, in most cases, the hand movement is minimal).

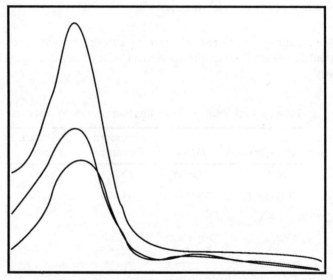

Figure 20. Fluent Fingerspelling (one repetition)

Figure 21 provides an interesting comparison. This is a plot of trial 13 (SMS), an example of non-fluent fingerspelling. A higher degree of non-synchronicity among individual articulators can be observed; the peak velocities do not overlap to the extent that was seen in Figure 20.

The difference is even more striking when velocity plots of repetitions are observed. Figure 22 shows trial 20 of subject TLS producing fluent fingerspelling. The synchronicity of the peak velocities of individual articulators is again apparent. In non-fluent repetitive fingerspelling, however, the same temporal variability de-

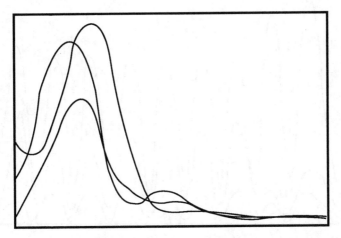

Figure 21. Non-Fluent Fingerspelling (one repetition)

scribed above appears. Figure 23 is a plot of non-fluent fingerspelling from trial 17; the non-simultaneity can be clearly observed. It should be noted that Figure 22 and Figure 23 represent plots of the same subject fingerspelling the same word. The productions occurred within 30 seconds of each other. The only difference is that trial 20 was fluent and trial 17 was non-fluent. Such synchronicity, if it is a significant feature of fluent fingerspelling, provides initial evidence of cooperativity among articulators and thus of an underlying dynamic organization to fingerspelling

A measure of temporal synchronicity was devised which evaluated the timing relations among the individual articulators. Figure 24 illustrates the technique used. The timings of the peak velocities for each of the three markers was noted. These times correspond to t_1, t_2, and t_3. The standard deviation of these three times was computed and used as a measure of temporal synchronicity. Thus, if the velocity peaks for all three markers occurred at exactly the same point in time, the temporal variability would be zero (perfectly synchronic); as the timings of the three velocity peaks vary, the standard deviation increases. This process was repeated for each set of peak velocities in the trial.[4] The set of temporal synchronicity values was then grouped according to fluent or non-fluent productions and a t-test applied to determine whether the two groups were significantly different.

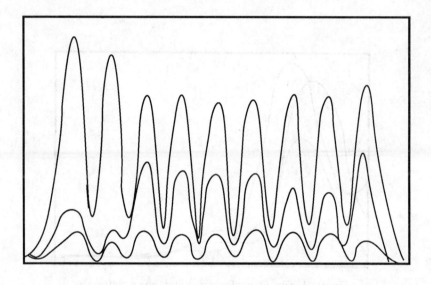

Figure 22. Fluent Fingerspelling (five repetitions)

The results for the measure of peak velocity timings are given in Table 24 (times are given in seconds).

In fluent fingerspelling, the timings of the peak velocities of each articulator showed an average temporal variability of 18.6 milliseconds. For the non-fluent fingerspelling data, the articulator timings showed an average variability of 40.3 milliseconds. A t-test indicates that the fluent and non-fluent groups are significantly different, $t = 3.77$, $p < .001$ (one-tail).[5]

Discussion

The results reported in this chapter support three broad conclusions. First, it is clear that speed, at least simply considered, is not an important point of control in the underlying organization of fingerspelling. When measured in terms of rate of letter production, the fluent words in this study were not produced significantly faster than the non-fluent words. Moreover, the fluent rate of 213 milliseconds per letter accords well with the average speed reported by other researchers. Thus, although these data

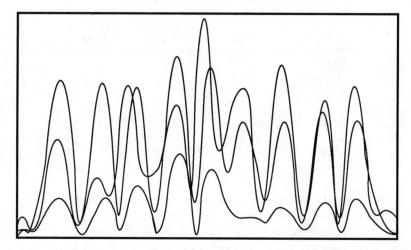

Figure 23. Non-Fluent Fingerspelling (five repetitions)

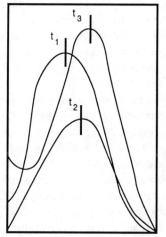

Figure 24. Measurement of Temporal Synchronicity

were collected under laboratory conditions, the data seem to be entirely representative of normal fingerspelling.

Table 24: t-Test Results, Peak Velocity Timings

Category	Mean	Standard Deviation	Standard Error
Fluent	.0186	.010	.002
Non-fluent	.0403	.028	.005

t Value	Degrees of Freedom	2-Tail Probability
-3.77	31	.001

When speed is measured in terms of the mean peak velocity of a moving articulator, the situation becomes more complex. In this case, fluent fingerspelling is different than non-fluent fingerspelling, but in the wrong direction. Rather than moving faster, the index finger in fluent fingerspelling moved with an average maximum velocity of 246 mm/sec, significantly slower than it moved in non-fluent fingerspelling at 343 mm/sec.

Secondly, the results point to peak velocity as a possible point of control. Interpreting these results in terms of the model proposed in the previous chapter provides further support for the notion that transitions are significant features of fingerspelling. Peak velocities occur at the point where an articulator's acceleration changes sign — that is, where positive acceleration becomes negative and vice versa. For fingerspelling data, these points occur midway through a motion. In terms of the model, they are the nucleus of the transitions in these simple words. Thus, these results provide one more source of evidence that transitions are likely to be a significant aspect in the organization of fingerspelling. This conclusion is further supported by other lines of evidence suggesting that "acceleration and its effects are likely candidates for perceptual importance" (Shaw and Cutting, 1980:77; see also Runeson, 1974; Summerfield et al., 1980).

Finally, both the peak velocity and the temporal synchronicity findings provide preliminary evidence for an underlying dynamic organization of fingerspelling production. One consequence of a dynamic view is that "real systems ... consist of ensembles of coupled and mutually entrained oscillators and that coordination is a natural consequence of this organization" (Kelso, Tuller, and Harris, 1983:140). Cooperativity, in this case, appears as the result of individual articulators working together in a functional grouping — a coordinative structure. When such cooperativity is not present, we predict that articulators will act in an independent, uncoordinated fashion. The data presented here support this prediction. In non-fluent fingerspelling, individual articulators act relatively independently of each other. Dynamic control is evidenced by the mutual entrainment or "mutual synchronization" (Turvey, 1980:53) of many independent articulators. In fluent fingerspelling, we see this when individual articulators are controlled so that they act as a unit both temporally and kinematically. In the terminology of dynamics, this phenomenon may be understood as the lowering of degrees of freedom in a complex, multi-degree of freedom system. The result is that the complex system is "coordinated to produce functionally-specific ordered behavior or spatiotemporal patterns" (Kelso and Schöner, to appear). Applied to the production and perception of fingerspelling, the result is that ensembles of independent articulators become functionally grouped and operate in a cooperative, coordinated manner in the service of a linguistic goal — the production of comprehensible, fingerspelled words.

Chapter 6
Future Directions in
Signed Language Research

The Linguistic Study of Fingerspelling

The linguistic study of ASL has flourished in the last two decades, contributing significantly not only to our knowledge of the grammar of this signed language but also to our general understanding of the human capacity for language (Bellugi & Studdert-Kennedy, 1980; Fromkin, 1988; Newport and Meier, 1985; Poizner, Klima, & Bellugi, 1987). Yet, one form of signed language, fingerspelling, has gone virtually unnoticed by researchers. We have very little empirical data on the acquisition, perception, and production of fingerspelling.

What could have caused this lack of interest in fingerspelling? Two explanations are possible. Early linguistic research on signed language was preoccupied with establishing ASL as a language in its own right, unrelated to any spoken language, and not merely a derivative of English. Fingerspelling clearly relates at some level to a spoken language — it is a derivative of English indirectly, through the secondary medium of written English. Thus, the linguistic study of fingerspelling did not fit within the agenda of the times.[1]

The second explanation concerns the theoretical assumption that the phonological structure of signed languages is primarily simultaneously, rather than sequentially, organized. Fingerspelling is clearly sequential. Even if the research agenda could have supported a study of fingerspelling, the accepted theoretical framework implied that fingerspelling is essentially different from signed languages and thus of little interest.

Times have changed, and both the research and theoretical climates are more conducive to the linguistic study of fingerspelling. ASL has firmly taken its place as a legitimate language; in fact, many colleges and universities now offer ASL in fulfillment of their foreign language requirements (Wilcox & Wilbers, 1987). The advent of sequential analyses of signed language phonology now motivates a theoretical re-evaluation of the structure of fingerspelling.

The common conception of fingerspelling is that it consists only of a sequence of handshapes which correspond to English letters. This simple cipher model of fingerspelling, while describing a necessary feature (the handshape/letter correspondence), is clearly inadequate to explain how fingerspelling is acquired by young deaf children or hearing adults. Hearing adults learning signed languages in a college setting, for example, feel that learning to understand fingerspelling is one of the most difficult tasks that they face. According to the students surveyed in this study, learning to understand fingerspelling is even more difficult than learning to understand ASL. The implication of this finding may not be immediately obvious, but it is tremendously important. Learning to fingerspelling is more like learning another language than learning a code for English.

Why is fingerspelling so difficult to perceive? In order to begin answering this question, we need a much more detailed understanding of the phonetic structure of fingerspelling. To understand why fingerspelling is so hard to see, we need to know more about what people are looking at. Fingerspelling is not merely a sequence of static, canonical forms, but a continuous signal in which the fingers are constantly moving towards targets which are rarely, if ever, unambiguously achieved. Even a simple exploration of the kinematics of fingerspelling demonstrates that most of the time spent in motion is not in a canonical handshape. The implication for comprehension is clear. If students are trying to perceive static, unambiguous handshape — the forms that they were probably taught in class — then it is little wonder why they find fingerspelling so difficult. They are looking for something that is not there. Deaf children acquiring fingerspelling as part of their first- language acquisition, on the other hand, do not approach the task with the preconception that fingerspelling is so organized. Consequently, they perceive fingerspelling more as complex "signs" — much the same as the normal route of language development in hearing children, who first acquire whole units (words, phrases, and formulaic expressions) and only later begin to manipulate the parts.

Studying what people are looking at in kinematic terms is equivalent to describing fingerspelling at the phonetic level. We will not want to stop at this level; an understanding of how fingerspelling is organized and controlled as a system is the next logical step. The kinematic studies reported here also were intended to point the way towards the development of a dynamic model of fingerspelling.

Limitations and Suggestions for Further Study

Motion Analysis of Signed Language

The measurement of fingerspelling movements presents the researcher with many special challenges. Under ideal conditions, words would be chosen which clearly incorporate the movements under investigation. These movements would be monitored and the resulting movements measured. Several obstacles were encountered in the present study which made operating under such conditions impossible.

First, as noted in chapter 3, the laboratory arrangements could not be adjusted. This required selecting words which could be adequately monitored under the existing arrangement. In addition, certain constraints imposed by the equipment itself had to be taken into consideration. Since WATSMART is an optical monitoring system, it was critical that all three markers be visible to both cameras. Even though WATSMART software can perform splining procedures to interpolate for missing data, substantial obstruction of the markers necessarily results in loss of data. This also, therefore, limited which words could be used and where the markers could be placed.

Part of the problem is the fact that WATSMART is not a truly non-intrusive system; the markers themselves imposed certain limitations. The markers had to be attached to the subject's hand and the wires connecting the markers to the host computer had to be taped to the arm. The base of the markers was a plastic cup approximately 10 millimeters in diameter. Together with the mounting material, this formed a substantial addition to the subject's fingers. Although motion was not restricted by the attachment of markers, words had to be carefully chosen so that they would not be formed in a way which would either be impaired by the markers or risk obscuring or detaching a marker. Of course, naturalness also has to be considered; not only did the subjects have equipment attached to them, but they were in a laboratory situation.

A second and more serious limitation of WATSMART is the lack of a visual record. WATSMART data consist only of two-dimensional coordinates, represented as values in a data-file. These values can be plotted and manipulated in various ways (filtered, differentiated, and so forth), but they do not represent a visual record of the motion. Without a visual record of the item produced, it was difficult to know exactly when a fingerspelling movement (as opposed to random movement) began and to relate the very precise values obtained from WATSMART with a signer's sense of what "really counts" in fingerspelling. In addition, several studies could not be conducted because certain variables, such as timings of specific gestures (orientation changes, for example), could not be identified from the data plots alone. It should be noted that the problem was not that the data itself was inadequate, but rather that without a visual record of the actual movement the data could not be properly interpreted.

Other tracking systems exist which may be able to overcome these limitations. One such system relies on high-speed (frame-rates of 60, 200, or 2000 Hz), shuttered video-cameras which track multiple targets (Greaves, Wilson, and Walton, 1985). The targets can be identified by any of three methods: explicit, active light sources (such as light- emitting diodes); cooperative by passive targets (such as reflective tape); or totally passive targets (parts of the image which are inherently bright or dark with respect to the background). With this system, precise kinematic data can be collected, while still allowing the researcher to view the actual movements either at actual or slow- motion speeds.

A second system translates hand and finger movements directly into electrical signals (Foley, 1987). The subject wears a specially-equipped glove, called a Data-Glove©, which contains fiber-optic cables running the length of each finger and thumb. An LED sends light down the cables to a phototransistor at the other end. The fiber-optic cables are specially treated so that light escapes when the fingers flex; the greater the movement is, the more light is lost. The phototransistor converts these light signals to electrical signals which are then transmitted to a computer. Coupled with another device on the back of the glove which can sense absolute position and orientation, the glove provides a direct, non-intrusive way of tracking fingerspelling movements. This system present an added advantage to the researcher. Graphic images of the hand can be generated on a computer using data supplied by the glove. These images can then be used as is, or manipulated on various ways (with the addition of noise, deletion of portions of the movements, etc.) in further psycholinguistic perceptual studies of fingerspelling. Such a device has been used recently to develop a communication aid for use by deaf and deaf-blind persons which translates fingerspelling motions (finger angles) to synthesized-speech.

Learning to Fingerspell

Acquisition of fingerspelling, especially learning to comprehend fingerspelling, is not easy for hearing adult learners. It is not the same as learning a static handshape/letter cipher for English. What is it about fingerspelling that makes it so difficult?

First, we need to know what students are looking for — what is their perceptual strategy for comprehending fingerspelling? We know that looking for individual letters is probably not the best strategy. Fingerspelled words are better understood as something "more than the sum of their parts." Still, a whole unit cannot be seen unless one has seen at least some of its constitutive parts. In other words, the problem may not be that students must see whole words and not the parts that make up the whole word, but that they are expecting the wrong parts. Expecting to see perfectly formed, largely static handshapes is tantamount to searching for the wrong part. Transitional movements, as we have seen, may carry a substantial portion of the information load in fingerspelling.

The temporal entrainment results support this conclusion. Perceptual judgments of fluency are made at points where changes in sign (from negative to positive and vice versa) in an articulator's acceleration occur. Acceleration changes sign (positive/negative) midway through a movement between two targets — at the center of the transition.

A preliminary discussion of the problem with fingerspelling students has led to a similar conclusion. When they critique theirs and other's fingerspelling in an effort to discover what makes it difficult to understand, they report two general problems: lack of letter definition, and lack of word definition (in multi-word utterances). In both of these cases, but especially in the case of letter definition, the problem is not that they expect the fingerspeller to stop moving after each letter; rather, there is a sense that the movements between letters lacks "snap" (again, we must resort to subjective terms).

Future studies should continue in two directions. First, students and proficient fingerspellers could be used to obtain reliable ratings about the ease or difficulty of understanding various styles of fingerspelling. Then, these different styles could be analyzed to find the kinematic variables that seem to consistently identify good versus poor fingerspelling. Although fluency was not a major focus of this paper, studies of fluent versus non-fluent fingerspellers afford the potential for contributing enormously to our understanding both of production and perception of fingerspelling. Naturally, studies of this type require the capability of viewing the actual movements that are being tracked and analyzed.

Models of Fingerspelling

The model of fingerspelling presented in chapter 4 is tentative at best. Several studies can be suggested which would extend and revise this model.

One of the most serious limitations of the study was the *ad hoc* way in which the beginnings and ends of targets and transitions were determined. This was necessitated mainly because of equipment limitations. Future studies should, however, attempt to remedy this situation by determining in a more principled way where targets begin and end. High-speed videotape, such as the system described above, could enable the researcher to do this by presenting single frames from various points along the trajectory to a group of viewers. Identification procedures could be used to determine when the salience of the handshape reached the level where subjects could accurately identify the target. These points could then be used as the beginning and end points of the target, and the portion between them as the transitions.

Another limitation concerns the restricted data used in this study. Although the procedures used in this study collected 2,250 data points per second, these data represent only three subjects producing a restricted set of fingerspelled words. Finally, this study has claimed that a dynamic model of fingerspelling is possible, and preliminary evidence was offered in support of this claim. Future studies should focus on testing predictions which the dynamic model makes concerning the organization of fingerspelling.

One prediction made by dynamic models is that a challenge or perturbation to one or more members of a functional grouping of articulators, a coordinative structure, will be responded to by other, non-mechanically linked members of the group. The bite-block experiments cited in chapter 4 offer evidence that such an organization is present in speech (Kelso, Tuller, Vatikiotis-Bateson, and Fowler, 1984). Experimental data indicating that fingerspelling articulators react in the same way would provide evidence in support of the dynamic model.

An interesting corollary to this type of experiment could be conducted using fingerspelling and speech. There is a popular method of communicating, called simultaneous communication, or SimCom, in which signers speak and sign (including fingerspelling) at the same time[2]. It has often been suggested that SimCom is more than the mere simultaneous production of a language in two modalities. Simultaneous communication imposes new and unique processing demands on its users (Baker, 1978; Maxwell, 1990).

Dynamic modeling offers both a way to understand SimCom and a test of the prediction that coordinative structures — in this case functional groupings of articulators across linguistic modalities — behave cooperatively. The prediction is that speech articulators and sign articulators will form a coordinative structure and act as a unit. In the words of dynamic theory, "when an individual speaks and moves at the same time, the degrees of freedom are constrained such that the system is parameterized as a total unit" (Kelso, Tuller, and Harris, 1983:151). A perturbation to one of the speech articulators or one of the signing articulators would result in a cooperative reaction from other, non-mechanically linked, articulators.

Another prediction of dynamic theory is that certain variables will remain invariant across transformations in the production. In speech, evidence has been offered that relative timing among articulators remains constant across substantial changes in duration and amplitude of articulator activity such as occur when a speaker varies her speaking rate and stress pattern (evidence from linguistic but nonspeech tasks, and from non-linguistic motor tasks also exists, see Viviani and Ter-zuolo, 1980; Grillner, 1975). Future studies of fingerspelling should focus on varying fingerspelling rate and stress patterns in the search for invariant patterns of organi-zation.

Sign Science and Speech Science: The Search for Unity

The British physicist, Paul Davies, once remarked that "all science is the search for unity" (Davies, 1984:6). The science of dynamics, and the allied field of synergetics, has provided researchers with powerful tools for exploring unity across a wide range of physical, biological, chemical and biochemical, sociological, and linguistic systems (Abraham and Shaw, 1982; Haken, 1977, 1985). Signed languages, not only com-monly recognized primary languages such as American Sign Language but also rep-resentations in the signed modality such as fingerspelling, provide researchers with a unique setting into which we can extend the search for unity.

"If nature operates with ancient themes, as we suspect, then the same laws/strat-egies should appear at every level of description, and despite differences in material structure" (Kelso and Scholz, 1985:146–147). It has been common in the past to con-ceive of signed languages as very different than spoken languages. Throughout most of history, signed languages were not even thought to be languages. This view was discarded only in the face of massive evidence to the contrary. Later, linguists claimed that signed and spoken languages were critically different in their phonolog-ical structure. Spoken languages, they argued, are primarily sequential in their un-derlying organization, but signed languages exhibit a simultaneous sublexical structure. As we have seen, even this conception is now being questioned. Indeed, the entire course of thinking which contrasts signed and spoken languages has been one of positing differences, only to find that on closer inspection the differences are in-significant, or, considered on a different level of description, do not even exist.

These findings raise two questions. First, what is the relationship between spo-ken and signed languages? Are signed languages merely analogues of spoken lan-guages, the linguistic equivalent of the bat's wing (evolved quite differently from the bird's wing)? Or are they true homologues, biologically related, as the human lung is to the swim bladder of fish?

The results of the studies reported here suggest that it may be possible to frame the study of signed languages and spoken languages in terms that will lead to answers to this question of relationship. Specifically, they suggest a model that describes both spoken and signed languages as *gestures*.

Second, what can the study of signed languages tell us about the human capacity for language? Linguists have not hesitated to propose theories of "human language" based solely on data drawn from spoken languages. By considering all human languages — both spoken and signed — we can gain a better understanding of how language is organized in the human brain (Poizner, Klima & Bellugi, 1987; see also the review by Kimura, 1988). The model that encompasses both spoken and signed languages assumes that the key lies in describing both with a single vocabulary, the vocabulary of neuromuscular activity.

Speech as Gestures

Oddly, much more work has been done describing speech than signing in gestural terms. Ulrich Neisser (1976), noted that it is possible to describe speech as "articulatory gesturing, and to treat speech perception as comparable to perceiving gestures of other kinds." Studdert-Kennedy (1987) has suggested that speech can be characterized as "subtly interleaved patterns of movements, coordinated across articulators." Indeed, an entire branch of the field of speech science is primarily concerned with the analysis of speech as gestures.

The description of speech as gestures contrasts with more traditional analyses of speech in terms of abstract linguistic units such as segments or syllables. In the traditional framework, the units of language — segments, for example — have three properties: they are discrete, static, and context-free. Speech is seen to consist of the sequential ordering of vocal tract states or targets.

Problems develop when we consider how these abstract linguistic units are realized as articulations. First, speech as actually produced is not discrete and context-free. Coarticulation results in segments influencing each other in complex, context dependent ways.

Second, the vocal tract is rarely, if ever, in a position of stasis. As noted by Fowler (1985), "if segments are only *achievements* of vocal tract states ... then most of the talking process involves getting to segments and less of it is involved in actually producing them."

Problems also arise in perception — it seems that we do not always perceive static targets. In experiments conducted by Strange (1987) sequences of segments, typically consonant-vowel-consonant (CVC) sequences, were manipulated to test whether perceivers rely on information for canonical "target" formant frequencies or transitions. Because of coarticulation there is a period of time during the transition from C to V and from V to C when the segments influence one another. Strange took a word such as *bab*, electronically attenuated to zero the middle two-thirds of the vowel (leaving in the surrounding consonants and the coarticulated transitions), and asked subjects to identify the vowel. Subjects had no more difficulty doing this than when the vowel was left intact. On the other hand, when the coarticulated transitions were reduced to silence and the middle two-thirds of the vowel left intact, subjects experienced difficulty identifying the *vowel*. The results led Strange to propose a model of speech perception in which vowels are characterized as gestures, the acoustic consequences of which are perceptually relevant.

Fowler's (1987) synthesis of these findings from speech production and perception provides an insight into how the results may apply to signed language. She suggests (1987:574) that "components of the phonology are essentially gestural, rather than being either postural as target theory proposes or than being even further abstracted from events at the articulatory surface as some theorists have asserted."

Fowler proposes that the best information for vowels is found in the changing, most coarticulated part of the acoustic signal. Two possible reasons are provided (Fowler 1987:577):

> One answer may be that listeners extract better information from acoustic consequences of the gestures that realize a segment than from the acoustic consequences of achievement of the gestures' target endpoints because segments are essentially gestural, not static, in nature. Another possibility, at least as interesting, is that the changing, most coarticulated parts of the signal are most informative because they best reveal coordinations of two important kinds: those among articulators responsible for producing a segment and those among the different articulatory systems responsible for producing overlapping segments.

The results reported in chapter 5 are clearly examples of similar principles operating in signed language. Fowler (1987:574–575) notes that "listeners focus on acoustic change, by hypothesis, because changing regions of the spectrum best reveal the gestural constituency of the talker's utterances." Rephrasing for signed language perception, we might hypothesize that signed language viewers focus on optical change (movement) because changing regions of the (optical) spectrum best reveal the gestural constituency of the signer's utterances.

Mowrey and Pagliuca (1988) have proposed a model of speech as gestures to account for phonetic evolution. In their model, words are "complexes of muscular gestures which are temporally ordered, but not in the serial segmental fashion familiar from classical [linguistic theory]." Rather than representing static or canonical vocal tract targets, their model represents the muscular activity which produces vocal tract movement. Their model clarifies a basic incompatibility between traditional (segmental) models of speech and its instantiation as neuromotor activity: "Bursts of muscular activity move the articulators along a trajectory and hence are more appropriate for describing the transitions between targets than the targets themselves. En-

listing the most dynamic aspects of articulation to describe the most static ends —
targets — mistakenly equates movement with stasis" (Mowrey & Pagliuca, 1988).

The Mowrey and Pagliuca model has been tested experimentally using electromyographic (EMG) measurement of speech errors. Speech errors are typically offered as strong evidence of the reality of segments (Fromkin, 1980). Mowrey and
MacKay (to appear) present evidence indicating that "individual muscular components of articulatory gestures are transposed in speech errors," thus contradicting
claims that language planning takes place at a segmental level.

Signing as Gestures

The notion that signed languages can be described in terms of muscular gestures
seems obvious. However, very little research has proceeded in this direction. A likely
explanation for this situation was already described at the beginning of this chapter:
signed language researchers often must argue for the status of signed languages as
human languages. Because of this, the thrust of much current signed language research has been to demonstrate that currently acceptable linguistic theories can be
applied to the study of signed languages. Signed language linguists have not, by and
large, been willing to explore theories seen as outside of the mainstream of linguistic
theory. While understandable, this conservatism is tenable only if the basic assumptions of theories of speech organization are correct. As we saw above, many researchers claim that they are not.

The result has been that much effort is spent attempting to locate the equiva-
lents of segments in signed languages. As we noted in chapter 1, linguists have proposed as candidates for signed segments movements and holds (Liddell, 1984a),
movements and locations (Sandler, 1986), and movements and positions (Perlmutter, 1990). Others have taken another tack and proposed that common ground between signed and spoken languages will be found at the level of the syllable (Wilbur,
1987). Still others have proposed that signed languages simply do not have segments
(Edmonson, 1987). So far, no one has seriously considered the possibility that signed
words, like spoken words, may be analyzed as complexes of temporally ordered neuromuscular gestures.

Figure 25 on page 89 shows a schematic representation of the similarities between spoken and signed language perception and production in a gestural model
(the figure is derived from Fowler & Smith, 1986). A few of the characteristics that
speech and fingerspelling share as gestures are outlined in Table 25 on page 90.

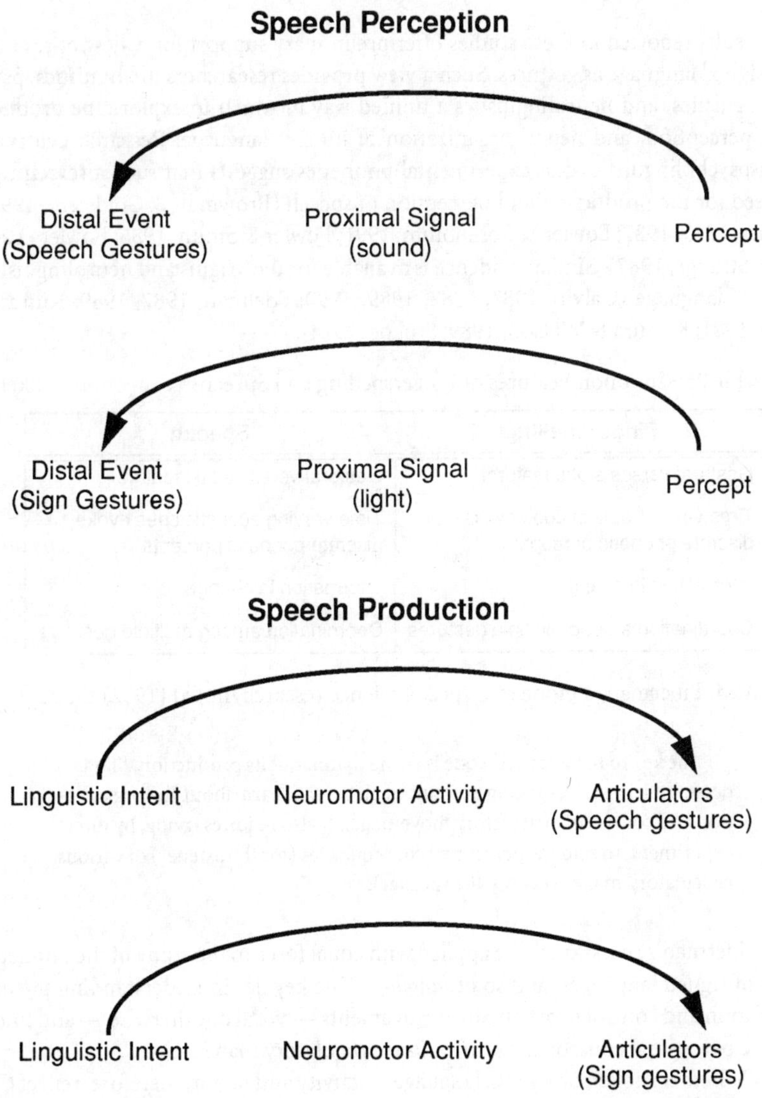

Speech Perception

Distal Event   Proximal Signal   Percept
(Speech Gestures)   (sound)

Distal Event   Proximal Signal   Percept
(Sign Gestures)   (light)

Speech Production

Linguistic Intent   Neuromotor Activity   Articulators
                                               (Speech gestures)

Linguistic Intent   Neuromotor Activity   Articulators
                                               (Sign gestures)

Figure 25. Sign and Spoken Language Perception and Production

Is Speech Special?

The results reported in these studies offer preliminary support for a view of spoken and signed language as gestures. Such a view provides researchers in linguistics, psycholinguistics, and neurolinguistics a unified way in which to explore the production, perception, and neural organization of human language. Research evidence from psycholinguistics and experimental phonetics suggests that such a search can succeed for the production and perception of speech (Browman & Goldstein, 1991; Fowler, 1985, 1987; Fowler & Rosenblum, 1991; Fowler & Smith, 1986; Fowler et al., 1980; Strange, 1987). Similar evidence is available for the origins and neurolinguistic basis of language (Calvin, 1983, 1987, 1989, 1990; Edelman, 1987, 1989; Kimura, 1976, 1981; Kimura & Watson, 1989; Stokoe, 1974).

Table 25: Common Features of Fingerspelling and Speech

Fingerspelling	Speech
Gestural versus static/featural	Gestural versus static/featural
Time varying optical cues evoke discrete phonetic percepts	Time varying acoustic cues evoke discrete phonetic percepts
Information in change	Information in change
Coordination among multiple gestures	Coordination among multiple gestures

A.M. Liberman, a pioneer in speech science research, noted (1982) that:

> the key to the phonetic code is in the manner of its production. [To understand it] requires taking account of all we can learn about the organization and control of articulatory movements. It also requires trying, by direct experiment, to find the perceptual consequences (for the listener) of various articulatory maneuvers (by the speaker).

Liberman's remarks can be applied with equal force to the study of the phonetic basis of signed languages, and so of *language*. The key lies in understanding the organization and control of articulatory movements — vocal or otherwise — and finding the perceptual consequences of various articulatory maneuvers.

"Whether spoken or signed, language is activity and might, therefore, reflect the organizational style that characterizes the control and coordination of acts" (Turvey, 1980:41). This book has attempted more than merely to provide a preliminary investigation of the phonetic structure of fingerspelling. It was motivated by a belief that differences attributed to the material structure of language may only reflect the level of description of our linguistic theories. Thus, it also was intended to inform and to explore a view of signed and spoken languages using the common vocabulary of articulatory gestures. According to this view, language is understood not as a mapping between meanings and sounds or meanings and signs, but more generally as a mapping between intentions and actions. In both signed and spoken languages, human actions produce gestures which communicate intentions.

Notes to Chapter One

1. Although the term 'sign language' is more common, 'signed language' will be used throughout this book. It is more compatible with 'spoken' and 'written', and it draws attention to the fact that signing is not a language but a modality.

2. Efforts are presently underway, however, to devise an orthography for ASL (McIntire et al., 1987). See also the discussion on pages 11–12.

3. Fingerspelling will be glossed with capital letters separated by hyphens.

4. The discussion of writing and signing systems given here is not meant to be thorough. It is, rather, merely a broad overview, the purpose of which is to bring out the similarities between writing systems and systems of representing English in the signed modality. For further and more detailed discussion of writing systems, see Gelb (1963); Wilbur (1987) presents a comprehensive description of several signed English systems.

5. This is not to say that ASL cannot nominalize a verb. Supalla and Newport (1978) have described in detail just such a device in ASL. The point is that this device cannot be used to correspond in any simple way with the English morpheme "-ment".

6. Loan signs are conventionally transcribed with the symbol # followed by a gloss of the English origin.

7. Of course, the term fluency can mean several things, and this no doubt complicates the problem. When used to describe fingerspelling production, fluency variously refers to smoothness, speed, and correct handshape formation. Combined with these production factors is a subjective evaluation of "ease of perception" which influences our judgment of whether or not a person is a "fluent" fingerspeller.

8. The names for the distinctive features are Reich's own, and are not described in any detail in his article. (1963); Wilbur (1987) presents a comprehensive description of several signed English systems.

Notes to Chapter Two

1. Pidgin Sign English is a variety of signed language which shares characteristics of ASL and English (Woodward, 1973b).

2. The survey on which these results are based only mentioned fingerspelling, not loan signs, further supporting the assumption that fingerspelling should be grouped with MCE.

3. The correlation coefficients of the survey rankings were used as a measure of similarity. The sign of the coefficient was retained, so the clusters are for positively correlated variables only; that is, variables that correlate negatively with a factor do not appear in the same cluster with variables that correlate positively (Norusis 1986:B-85).

Notes to Chapter Four

1. Fowler's proposal closely resembles a computer model of speech perception based on principles of interactive activation being developed by McClelland and Elman (1986).

2. Severe marker obstruction occurred on the data-files for subject BAH's production of B-U-T, as identified by WATSMART system software during the data reconstruction process. Therefore, no data from this subject was included in this study.

3. It should be pointed out that this measurement is being made on marker 3 (index finger) at a point distant from the tip of the finger. Thus, 1 millimeter of displacement, using this measurement, would be equivalent to a much larger displacement at the fingertip.

Notes to Chapter Five

1. This is not an ideal method for determining precise timings, since the peaks occur midway through the first and the last movements; in other words, this method systematically underestimates the time. It was used because locating the exact points where fingerspelled words begin and end with any degree of reliability was not possible. In any event, the degree of error is likely to be very small, since the data analyzed consisted of several repetitions of the same word.

2. Since the experimenter was the only person observing the subjects and WATSMART data carries no visual record, there is no way to test the reliability of the fluent/non-fluent distinction. It should be noted that the experimenter was a certified interpreter, a trained evaluator of interpreters for the Registry of Interpreters for the Deaf, and a fingerspelling instructor — in short, he was accustomed to making judgments of fluency of fingerspelling. The original log entries were made merely as a record of relevant factors in the data collection and not for a studied variable; thus, they are unlikely to be biased.

3. The timings were calculated by dividing the total time taken into the number of letters produced. For all but trial 16 of TLS the numerator was 15 (five trials of a three-letter word); trial 16 used a numerator of 12 (four trials of a three-letter word).

4. The method used here measured overall temporal variability and was not able to distinguish between random versus consistent timing differences. The distinction is between *synchronicity* and *entrainment*. "Synchronicity is that state which occurs when both frequency and phase of coupled oscillators are matched exactly; entrainment refers to the matching of frequencies, although one oscillator may lead or lag behind the other" (Kelso, Tuller, and Harris, 1983:159). For example, consider the case where one articulator consistently reaches a peak velocity 50 milliseconds before another. Since the difference is consistent, it should not be considered a lack of coordination. The current method would, however, treat this as temporal variability on par with the type of random variability which should be viewed as uncoordinated. It should be noted that while this may pose a problem for future studies which examine more complex words, there is no evidence of such phase differences in the present data. Thus, for these simple fingerspelled words, this method seems entirely adequate.

5. The probability reported in Table 9 is for a 2-tail test; however, since a prediction in one direction was theoretically motivated (non-fluent groups would show more variability), a 1-tail test is appropriate.

Notes to Chapter Six

1. The only linguistic study conducted during this period that related to fingerspelling was Battison's (1978) study of loan signs, where it was shown that words from one language (fingerspelled English) are borrowed into another (ASL).

2. Since it is not possible to produce two languages simultaneously, even when dual modalities would seem to allow it, signers must be using English in order to do SimCom.

References

Abraham, R. H. & C. D. Shaw. *Dynamics—the geometry of behavior.* Santa Cruz, CA: Aerial Press, 1982.

Akamatsu, C. T. The acquisition of fingerspelling in pre-school children. Unpublished doctoral dissertation, University of Rochester, 1982.

Akamatsu, C. T. Fingerspelling formulae: A word is more or less than the sum of its letters. In W. Stokoe and V. Volterra (Eds.), *SLR '83: sign language research.* Linstok Press, Silver Spring, MD: 1985.

Anderson, S. A. *The organization of phonology.* NY: Academic Press, 1974.

Anthony, D. *Seeing Essential English (Vols. 1 and 2).* Educational Services Division, Anaheim Union School District, Anaheim, CA, 1971.

Baker, C. How does 'Sim Com' fit into a bilingual approach to education? Paper presented at the Second National Symposium on Sign Language Research and Teaching, Coronado, CA, 1978.

Battison, R. Phonology in American Sign Language: 3-D and digit vision. Paper presented at the California Linguistic Association Conference, Stanford, CA, 1973.

Battison, R. Phonological deletion in American Sign Language. *Sign Language Studies,* 1974, 5, 1–19.

Battison, R. *Lexical borrowing in American Sign Language.* Silver Spring, MD: Linstok Press, 1978.

Battison, R., Markowicz, H. and J. Woodward. A good rule of thumb: Variable phonology in American Sign Language. In R. Shuy and R. Fasolds (Eds.), *New ways of analyzing variation in English II.* Washington, DC: Georgetown University Press, 1975.

Bellugi, U. & M. Studdert-Kennedy (Eds.). *Signed and spoken languages: Biological constraints on linguistic form.* Deerfield Beach, FL: Verlag Chemie, 1980.

Bloomfield, L. *Language.* NY: Holt, Rinehart and Winston, 1933.

Bornstein, H. *Reading the manual alphabet.* Washington, DC: Gallaudet College Press, 1965.

Bornstein, H. Sign languages in the education of the deaf. In I. M. Schlesinger & L. Namir (Eds.), *Sign language of the deaf.* Academic Press, NY: 1978.

Bornstein, H., Hamilton, L., Kannapell, B., Roy, H. & K. Saulnier. *Basic pre-school signed English dictionary.* Washington, DC: Gallaudet College, 1973.

Browman, C. P. & L. M. Goldstein. Dynamic modeling of phonetic structure. In V. Fromkin (Ed.), *Phonetic linguistics.* Academic Press, NY: 1985.

Browman, C. P. & L. M. Goldstein. Gestural structures: Distinctiveness, phonological processes, and historical change. In I.G. Mattingly & M. Studdert-Kennedy (Eds.), *Modularity and the motor theory of speech perception*. Hillsdale, NJ: Lawrence Erlbaum, 1991.

Burling, R. *Man's many voices: Language in its cultural context.* NY: Holt, Rinehart and Winston, Inc., 1970.

Cairns, C. and M. Feinstein. Syllable structure and the theory of markedness. *Linguistic Inquiry*, 1982, *13*, 193-225.

Calvin, W. H. A stone's throw and its launch window: Timing precision and its implications for language and hominid brains. *Journal of Theoretical Biology*, 1983, *104*, 121–135.

Calvin, W. H. The great encephalization: Throwing, juvenalization, developmental slowing, and material mortality roles in prehuman brain enlargement. *Human Ethology Newsletter*, 1987, *5(3)*, 4–6.

Calvin, W. H. *The cerebral symphony: Seashore reflections on the structure of consciousness.* NY: Bantam, 1989.

Calvin, W. H. *The ascent of mind:Ice age climates and the evolution of intelligence.* NY: Bantam, 1990.

Cornett, R. Cued speech. *American Annals of the Deaf*, 1967, *112*, 3 13.

Daniloff, R. G. and R. E. Hammarberg. On defining coarticulation. *Journal of Phonetics*, 1973, *1*, 239-248.

Davies, P. *Superforce.* NY: Simon and Schuster, 1984.

Dew, R. & P. J. Jensen. *Phonetic processing: The dynamics of speech.* Columbus, OH: Charles E. Merrill, 1977.

Edelman, G. *Neural Darwinism: The theory of neuronal group selection.* NY: Basic Books, 1987.

Edelman, G. *The remembered present: A biological theory of consciousness.* NY: Basic Books, 1989.

Edmondson, W. Segments in signed languages: Do they exist and does it matter. Paper presented at IV International Symposium on Sign Language Research, Finland, 1987.

Fischer, S. D. & P. Siple (Eds.). *Theoretical issues in sign language research (volume 1).* Chicago, IL: University of Chicago Press, 1990.

Foley, J. D. Interfaces for advanced computing. *Scientific American*, 1987, *257(4)*, 126-136.

Fowler, C. A. Coarticulation and theories of extrinsic timing. *Journal of Phonetics*, 1980, *8*, 113-133.

Fowler, C. A. Segmentation of coarticulated speech in perception. *Perception and Psychophysics*, 1984, *36(4)*, 359-368.

Fowler, C. A. Current perspectives on language and speech production: A critical overview. In R. G. Daniloff (Ed.), *Speech science: Recent advances*. San Diego: College Hill Press, 1985.

Fowler, C. A. Perceivers are realists, talkers too: Commentary on papers by Strange, Diehl et al., and Rakerd and Verbrugge. *Journal of memory and language*, 1987, *26*, 574–587.

Fowler, C. A. & L. D. Rosenblum. The perception of phonetic gestures. In I.G. Mattingly & M. Studdert-Kennedy (Eds.), *Modularity and the motor theory of speech perception*. Hillsdale, NJ: Lawrence Erlbaum, 1991.

Fowler, C. A. & M. R. Smith. Speech perception as "vector analysis": An approach to the problems of invariance and segmentation. In J. S. Perkell & D. H. Klatt (Eds.), *Invariance and variability in speech processes*. Hillsdale, NJ: Lawrence Erlbaum, 1986.

Fowler, C. A. and M. Turvey. Immediate compensation in bite-block speech. *Phonetica*, 1980, *37*, 306-326.

Fowler, C. A., Rubin, P., Remez, R. E. & M. T. Turvey. Implications for speech production of a general theory of action. In B. Butterworth (Ed.), *Language production (Vol. 1: Speech and talk)*. London: Academic Press, 1980.

Friedman, L. Phonology of a soundless language: Phonological structure of American Sign Language. Unpublished doctoral dissertation, University of California, Berkeley, 1976.

Fromkin, V. (Ed.). *Errors in linguistic performance: Slips of the tongue, ear, pen, and hand*. NY: Academic Press, 1980.

Fromkin, V. Sign languages: Evidence for language universals and the linguistic capacity of the human brain. *Sign Language Studies*, 1988, *59*, 115–127.

Fromkin, V. & R. Rodman. *An introduction to language*. NY: Holt, Rinehart, and Winston, 1974.

Fukson, O. I., Berkinblit, M. B., & A. G. Fel'dman. The spinal frog takes into account the scheme of its body during the wiping reflex. *Science*, 1980, *209*, 1261-1263.

Gelb, I. J. *A study of writing*. Chicago, IL: University of Chicago Press, 1963.

Greaves, J. O. B., Wilson, R. S. & J. S. Walton. A video-based image analysis system for rapid, non-intrusive collection and reporting of motion data. Proceedings of the 1985 Society for Experimental Mechanics Fall Conference on Experimental Mechanics, Grenelefe, FL, 1985.

Grillner, S. Locomotion in vertebrates. *Physiological Reviews*, 1975, *55*, 247-304.

Grosjean, F. and H. Lane (Eds.). *Recent perspectives on American Sign Language*. Hillsdale, NJ: Lawrence Erlbaum, 1980.

Guillory, L. M. *Expressive and receptive fingerspelling for hearing adults*. Baton Rouge, LA: Claitor's Publishing Division, 1966.

Gustason, G., Pfetzing, D. & E. Zawolkow. *Signing Exact English*. Rossmoor, CA: Modern Signs Press, 1972.

Haken, H. *Synergetics: An introduction*. Berlin: Springer-Verlag, 1977.

Haken, H. (Ed.), *Complex systems: Operational approaches in neurobiology, physics and computers*. Berlin: Springer-Verlag, 1985.

Haken, H., Kelso, J. A. S. & H. Bunz. A theoretical model of phase transitions in human hand movements. *Biological Cybernetics*, 1985, *51*, 347-356.

Hanson, V. L. When a word is not the sum of its letters: Fingerspelling and spelling. In F. Caccamise, M. Garretson, and U. Bellugi (Eds.), *Teaching American Sign Language as a Second/Foreign Language*. National Association of the Deaf, Silver Spring, MD: 1981.

Hanson, V. L., Liberman, I. Y., & D. Shankweiler. Linguistic coding by deaf children in relation to beginning reading success. *Journal of Experimental Child Psychology*, 1984, *37*, 378-393.

Henke, W. L. Dynamic articulatory model of speech production using computer simulation. Unpublished doctoral dissertation, MIT, 1966.

Hudson, R. A. *Sociolinguistics*. Cambridge, England: Cambridge University Press, 1980.

Kegl, J. and R. B. Wilbur. When does structure stop and style begin? Syntax, morphology, and phonology vs. stylistic variation in American Sign Language. Papers from the Twelfth Regional Meeting, Chicago Linguistic Society, Chicago, IL, 1976.

Kelso, J. A. S. Pattern formation in speech and limb movements involving many degrees of freedom. *Experimental Brain Research*, 1986, *15*, 105-128.

Kelso, J. A. S. & J. E. Clark (Eds.), *The development of movement control and coordination*. John Wiley, NY: 1982.

Kelso, J. A. S. & J. P. Scholz. Cooperative phenomena in biological motion. In H. Haken (Ed.), *Complex systems: Operational approaches in neurobiology, physics and computers*. Berlin: Springer-Verlag, 1985.

Kelso, J. A. S. & G. Schöner. Toward a physical (synergetic) theory of biological co-ordination. In R. Graham (Ed.), *Lasers and synergetics*. Berlin: Springer-Verlag, to appear.

Kelso, J. A. S. & B. Tuller. "Compensatory articulation" under conditions of reduced afferent information: A dynamic formulation. *Journal of Speech and Hearing Research*, 1983, *26*, 217-224.

Kelso, J. A. S. & B. Tuller. A dynamical basis for action systems. In M. S. Gazzinaga (Ed.), *Handbook of cognitive neuroscience*. Plenum, NY: 1984.

Kelso, J. A. S., Holt, K. C., & A. E. Flatt. The role of proprioception in the perception and control of human movement: Toward a theoretical reassessment. *Perception and Psychophysics*, 1980, *28*, 45-52.

Kelso, J. A. S., Saltzman, E. L. & B. Tuller. The dynamical perspective on speech production: data and theory. *Journal of Phonetics*, 1986, *14*, 29-59.

Kelso, J. A. S., Tuller, B., & K. S. Harris. A "dynamic pattern" perspective on the control and coordination of movement. In P. F. MacNeilage (Ed.), *The production of speech*. Springer-Verlag, NY: 1983.

Kelso, J. A. S., Tuller, B., Vatikiotis-Bateson, E., & C. A. Fowler. Functionally specific articulatory cooperation following jaw perturbations during speech: Evidence for coordinative structures. *Journal of Experimental Psychology: Human Perception and Performance*, 1984, *10(6)*, 812-832.

Kelso, J. A. S., Vatikiotis-Bateson, E., Saltzman, E. L., & B. Kay. A qualitative dynamic analysis of reiterant speech production: Phase portraits, kinematics, and dynamic modeling. *Journal of the Acoustic Society of America*, 1985, *77(1)*, 266-280.

Kent, R. D. Some considerations in the cineflourographic analysis of tongue movements during speech. *Phonetica*, 1972, *26*, 16-32.

Kimura, D. The neural basis of language qua gesture. In Whitaker & Whitaker (Eds.), *Studies in neurolinguistics*. NY: Academic Press, 1976.

Kimura, D. Neural mechanisms in manual signing. *Sign Language Studies*, 1981, *33*, 291-312.

Kimura, D. Review of Poizner et al., *What the hands reveal about the brain*, in *Language & Speech*, 1988, *31*, 375-378. [Reprinted in *Sign Language Studies*, 1990, *66*, 79-84 as "How special is language?"]

Kimura, D. & N. Watson. The relation between oral movement control and speech, *Brain and Language*, 1989, *37*, 565-590.

Klima, E. & U. Bellugi. *The signs of language*. Cambridge, MA: Harvard University Press, 1979.

Krashen, S. *The input hypothesis: Issues and implications*. NY: Longman, 1985.

Kuehn, D. P. & K. L. Moll. A cineradiographic study of VC and CV articulatory velocities. *Journal of Phonetics*, 1976, *4*, 303-320.

Kugler, P. N., Kelso, J. A. S., & M. T. Turvey. On the concept of coordinative structures as dissipative structures: Empirical lines of convergency. In G. E. Stelmach & J. Requin (Eds.), *Tutorials in motor behavior*. North Holland Publishing Co., NY: 1980a.

Kugler, P. N., Kelso, J. A. S., & M. T. Turvey. On the concept of coordinative structures as dissipative structures: Theoretical line. In G. E. Stelmach & J. Requin (Eds.), *Tutorials in motor behavior*. North Holland Publishing Co., NY: 1980b.

Kugler, P. N., Kelso, J. A. S., & M. T. Turvey. On the control and co-ordination of naturally developing systems. In J. A. S. Kelso & J. E. Clark (Eds.), *The development of movement control and coordination*. John Wiley, NY: 1982.

Lane, H., Boyes-Braem, P., & U. Bellugi. Preliminaries to a distinctive feature analysis of handshape in American Sign Language. *Cognitive Psychology*, 1976, *8*, 263-289.

Langacker, R. *Fundamentals of linguistic analysis*. NY: Harcourt Brace Jovanovich, 1972.

Liberman, A. M. On finding that speech is special. *American Psychologist*, 1982, *37(2)*, 148–167.

Liberman, A. M., Cooper, F. S., Shankweiler, D. P. & M. Studdert-Kennedy. Perception of the speech code. *Psychological Review*, 1967, *74*, 431-461.

Liddell, S. K. THINK and BELIEVE: Sequentiality in American Sign Language. *Language*, 1984a, *(64)2*, 372-399.

Liddell, S. K. Unrealized inceptive aspect in American Sign Language. Chicago Linguistic Society, 1984b.

Liddel, S. K. Structures for representing handshape and local movement at the phonemic level. In S. D. Fischer & P. Siple (Eds.), *Theoretical issues in sign language research*. Chicago, IL: University of Chicago Press, 1990.

Liddell, S. K. & R. E. Johnson. American Sign Language compound formation processes, lexicalization, and phonological remnants. *Natural Language and Linguistic Theory*, 1986, *4*, 445-513.

Liddell, S. K. & R. E. Johnson. American Sign Language: The phonological base. *Sign Language Studies*, 1989, *64*, 195–278.

Lindblom, B. & J. Sundberg. Acoustical consequences of lip, tongue, jaw, and larynx movement. *Journal of the Acoustical Society of America*, 1971, *50*, 1166-1179.

Locke, J. L. & V. L. Locke. Deaf children's phonetic, visual, and dactylic coding in a grapheme recall task. *Journal of Experimental Psychology*, 1971, *89*, 142-146.

MacNeilage, P. F. Motor control and serial ordering of speech. *Psychological Review*, 1970, *77*, 183-196.

MacNeilage, P. F. (Ed.), *The production of speech*. Springer-Verlag, NY: 1983.

Mandel, M. A. Natural constraints in sign language phonology: Data from anatomy. *Sign Language Studies*, 1979, *24*, 215-229.

Mandel, M. A. Phonotactics and morphophonology in American Sign Language. Unpublished doctoral dissertation, University of California, Berkeley, 1981.

Maxwell, M. Simultaneous communication: The state of the art and proposals for change. *Sign Language Studies*, 1990, *69*, 333–390.

McClelland, J. L. & J. L. Elman. The TRACE model of speech perception. *Cognitive Psychology*, 1986, *18*, 1-86.

McIntire, M. The acquisition of American Sign Language hand configurations. *Sign Language Studies*, 1977, 16, 247-266.

McIntire, M., Newkirk, D., Hutchins, S., and H. Poizner. Hands and faces: A preliminary inventory for written ASL. *Sign Language Studies*, 1987, *56*, 197-241.

Meirovitch, L. *Introduction to dynamics and control.* NY: John Wiley & Sons, 1985.

Mowl, G. *Fingerspelling and numbers: A student workbook in sign language.* Cresson, PA: Sign Language Video Tape Store, 1983.

Mowrey, R. & I.R.A. MacKay. Phonological primitives: electromyographic speech error evidence. To appear, *Journal of the Acoustic Society of America.*

Mowrey, R. & W. Pagliuca. The reductive character of phonetic evolution. Unpublished manuscript, 1988.

Neisser, U. *Cognition and reality: Principles and implications of cognitive psychology.* NY: Freeman, 1976.

Newport, E. L. & R. P. Meier. The acquisition of American Sign Language. In D. I. Slobin (Ed.), *The crosslinguistic study of language acquisition, Vol. I: The data.* Hillsdale, NY: Lawrence Erlbaum, 1985.

Norusis, M. J. *SPSS/PC+ Advanced statistics for the IBM PC/XT/AT.* Chicago, IL: SPSS Inc., 1986.

Padden, C. & B. LeMaster. An alphabet on hand: Acquisition of fingerspelling in deaf children. *Sign Language Studies*, 1985, *47*, 161-172.

Padden, C. & D. M. Perlmutter. American Sign Language and the architecture of phonological theory. *Natural Language & Linguistic Theory*, 1987, *5*, 335–76.

Parush, A., Ostry, D. J. & K. G. Munhall. A kinematic study of lingual coarticulation in VCV sequences. *Journal of the Acoustic Society of America*, 1983, *74(4)*, 1115-1125.

Pearson, K. G. The control of walking. *Scientific American*, 1976, 235, 72-79.

Perlmutter, D.M. On the segmental representation of transitional and bidirectional movements in American Sign Language phonology. In S. D. Fischer & P. Siple (Eds.), *Theoretical issues in sign language research*. Chicago, IL: University of Chicago Press, 1990.

Peters, A. *The units of language acquisition*. NY: Cambridge University Press, 1983.

Poizner, H. Perception of movement in American Sign Language: Effects of linguistic structure and linguistic experience. *Perception and Psychophysics*, 1983, *33(3)*, 215-231.

Poizner, H., Bellugi, U., & V. Lutes-Driscoll. Perception of American Sign Language in dynamic point-light displays. *Journal of Experimental Psychology: Human Perception and Performance*, 1981, *7(2)*, 430-440.

Poizner, H., Klima, E. S. & U. Bellugi. *What the hands reveal about the brain*. Cambridge, MA: MIT Press, 1987.

Poizner, H., Newkirk, D. & U. Bellugi. Processes controlling human movement: Neuromotor constraints on American Sign Language. *Journal of Motor Behavior*, 1983, *15(1)*, 2-18.

Poizner, H., Klima, E. S., Bellugi, U. & R. B. Livingston. Motion analysis of grammatical processes in a visual-gestural language. In N. I. Badler & J. K. Tsotsos (Eds.), *Motion: Representation and perception*. North-Holland, NY: 1986.

Reich, P. A. Visible distinctive features. In A. Makkai & V. B. Makkai (Eds.), *First LACUS Forum*. Hornbeam Press, Columbia, SC: 1975.

Reich, P. A. & M. Bick. An empirical investigation of some claims made in support of visible English. *American Annals of the Deaf*, 1976, *121(6)*, 573-577.

Reich, P. A. & M. Bick. How visible is visible English? *Sign Language Studies*, 1977, *14*, 59-72.

Repp, B. Dichotic competition of speech sounds: The role of acoustic stimulus structure. *Journal of Experimental Psychology: Human Perception and Performance*, 1977, *3*, 37-50.

Richards, J. T. & V. L. Hanson. Visual and production similarity of the handshapes of the American manual alphabet. *Perception and Psychophysics*, 1985, 38(4), 311-319.

Runeson, J. S. Constant velocity - not perceived as such. *Psychological Research*, 1974, *37*, 3-23.

Sandler, W. The spreading hand autosegment of American Sign Language. *Sign Language Studies*, 1986, *50*, 1-28.

Sandler, W. *Sequentiality and simultaneity in American Sign Language phonology.* Dordrecht: Foris, 1989.

Sandler, W. Temporal aspects and American Sign Language phonology. In S. D. Fischer & P. Siple (Eds.), *Theoretical issues in sign language research.* Chicago, IL: University of Chicago Press, 1990.

Sears, F. W. & M. W. Zemansky. *University physics.* Reading, MA: Addison-Wesley, Inc., 1949.

Shaw, R. E. & J. E. Cutting. Clues from an ecological theory of event perception. In U. Bellugi & M. Studdert-Kennedy (Eds.), *Signed and spoken languages: Biological constraints on linguistic form.* Deerfield Beach, FL: Verlag Chemie, 1980.

Siple, P. (Ed.). *Understanding language through sign language research.* NY: Academic Press, 1978.

Stokoe, W. C. *Sign language structure.* Silver Spring, MD: Linstok Press, 1960 [reprinted 1978].

Stokoe, W. C. Motor signs as the first form of language. In G. Hewes (Ed.), *Language origins.* Silver Spring, MD: Linstok Press, 1974.

Stokoe, W. C., Casterline, D. C. & C. G. Croneberg. *A dictionary of American Sign Language on linguistic principles.* Silver Spring, MD: Linstok Press, 1965 [reprinted 1976].

Strange, W. Information for vowels in formant transitions. *Journal of memory and language*, 1987, *26*, 550–557.

Studdert-Kennedy, M. The phoneme as a perceptualmotor structure. In A. Allport et. al. (Eds.), *Language perception and production: Relationships between listening, speaking, reading, and writing.* NY: Academic Press, 1987.

Stungis, J. Identification and discrimination of handshape in American Sign Language. *Perception and Psychophysics*, 1981, *29(3)*, 261-276.

Summerfield, A. Q., Cutting, J. E., Frishberg, F., Lane, H., Lindblom, B. E. F., Runeson, J. S., Shaw, R. E., Studdert-Kennedy, M. & M. T. Turvey. The structuring of language by the requirements of motor control and perception: Group Report. In U. Bellugi & M. Studdert-Kennedy (Eds.), *Signed and spoken languages: Biological constraints on linguistic form.* Deerfield Beach, FL: Verlag Chemie, 1980.

Supalla, T. and E. Newport. How many seats in a chair? The derivation of nouns and verbs in American Sign Language. In P. Siple (Ed.), *Understanding language through sign language research.* Academic Press, NY: 1978.

Turvey, M. T. Clues from the organization of motor systems. In U. Bellugi & M. Studdert-Kennedy (Eds.), *Signed and spoken languages: Biological constraints on linguistic form.* Deerfield Beach, FL: Verlag Chemie, 1980.

Tweney, R. D. Sign language and psycholinguistic process: Fact, hypotheses, and implications for interpretation. In D. Gerver & H. W. Sinaiko (Eds.), *Interpretation and communication.* NY: Plenum, 1978.

Van Cleve, J. V. (Ed.). *Gallaudet encyclopedia of deaf people and deafness.* NY: McGraw-Hill, 1987.

Viviani, P. & V. Terzuolo. Space-time invariance in learned motor skills. In G. E. Stelmach & J. Requin (Eds.), *Tutorials in motor behavior.* Amsterdam: North Holland, 1980.

Wallace, S. A. The coding of location: A test of the target hypothesis. *Journal of Motor Behavior,* 1977, *9(2),* 157-169.

Wampler, D. *Linguistics of Visual English.* Santa Rosa, CA: Early Childhood Education Department, Aurally Handicapped Program, Santa Rosa City Schools, 1971.

Wilbur, R. B. A multi-tiered theory of syllable structure for American Sign Language. Paper presented at the Annual Meeting, Linguistic Society of America, San Diego, CA, 1982.

Wilbur, R. B. The role of contact in the phonology of ASL. Paper presented at the Annual Meeting, Linguistic Society of America, Seattle, WA, 1985.

Wilbur, R. B. *American Sign Language: Linguistic and applied dimensions.* San Diego, CA: Little, Brown and Co., 1987.

Wilbur, R. B. Why syllables? What the notion means for American Sign Language research. In S.D. Fischer & P. Siple (Eds.), *Theoretical issues in sign language research.* Chicago, IL: University of Chicago Press, 1990.

Wilcox, S. & S. Wilbers. The case for academic acceptance of American Sign Language. *The Chronical of Higher Education,* July 1, 1987:30.

Woodward, J. Implicational lects on the deaf diglossic continuum. Unpublished doctoral dissertation, Georgetown University, Washington, DC, 1973a.

Woodward, J. Some characteristics of Pidgin Sign English. *Sign Language Studies,* 1973b, *3,* 39-46.

Zakia, R. D. & R. N. Haber. Sequential letter and word recognition in deaf and hearing subjects. *Perception and Psychophysics,* 1971, *9(1B),* 110-114.

Index

S
Synchronicity 72, 94
Synergetics 85

W
WATSMART
  data analysis 43
  hardware 37
  software 39

In the STUDIES IN SPEECH PATHOLOGY AND CLINICAL LINGUISTICS (SSPCL) series (Series Editors: Martin J. Ball and Raymond D. Kent) the following volumes have been published thus far, and will be published during 1992:

1. KENT, Raymond D.: *Intelligibility in Speech Disorders: Theory, Measurement and Management.* Amsterdam/Philadelphia, 1992.
2. CLAHSEN, Harald: *Child Language and Developmental Dysphasia: Linguistic Studies of the Acquisition of German.* (translated by Karin Richman) Amsterdam/Philadelphia, 1991.
3. WRAY, Alison: *The Focusing Hypothesis: The Theory of Left Hemisphere Lateralised Language Re-examined.* Amsterdam/Philadelphia, 1992. n.y.p.
4. WILCOX, Sherman: *The Phonetics of Fingerspelling.* Amsterdam/Philadelphia, 1992.

p.34 ref 8   p. 47 caption errors.

p 46
sus

p. 57 q. on fs, applies =ly to SL